Best of the
PACIFIC CREST TRAIL

WASHINGTON
55 Hikes

Best of the
PACIFIC CREST TRAIL

WASHINGTON
55 Hikes

DAN A. NELSON

THE
MOUNTAINEERS

Published by
The Mountaineers
1001 SW Klickitat Way, Suite 201
Seattle, WA 98134

First printing 2000, second printing 2004

Published simultaneously in Great Britain by Cordee, 3a DeMontfort Street, Leicester, England, LE1 7HD

Manufactured in the United States of America

Project Editor: Christine Ummel Hosler
Editor: Jane Crosen
Maps by Debbie Newell
All photographs by Dan A. Nelson
Cover design by Kristy L. Welch
Book design and layout by Kristy L. Welch

Cover photograph: *Goat Rocks Near Goat Lake* © 1997 Dan A. Nelson
Frontispiece: *A Pacific Crest Trail sign near Glacier Peak*

Library of Congress Cataloging-in-Publication Data

Nelson, Dan A.
  Best of the Pacific Crest Trail, Washington : 55 hikes / Dan A.
Nelson.—1st ed.
      p. cm.
Includes index.
  ISBN 0-89886-703-7 (pbk.)
  1. Hiking—Pacific Crest Trail—Guidebooks. 2. Pacific Crest
Trail—Guidebooks. I. Title.
  GV199.42.P3 N45 2000
  917.9—dc21   99-050669
                                                CIP

CONTENTS

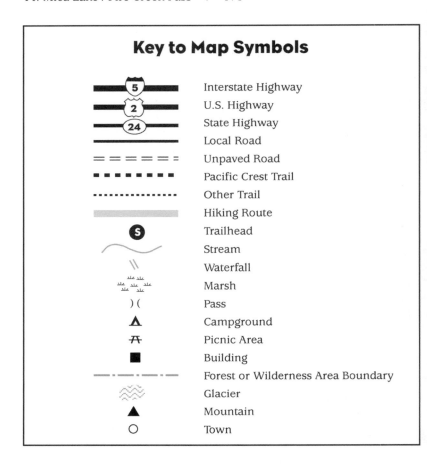

Key to Map Symbols

5	Interstate Highway
2	U.S. Highway
24	State Highway
———	Local Road
= = = = = =	Unpaved Road
■ ■ ■ ■ ■ ■	Pacific Crest Trail
• • • • • • •	Other Trail
▬▬▬	Hiking Route
S	Trailhead
~	Stream
\\	Waterfall
⁂	Marsh
) (	Pass
▲	Campground
⊼	Picnic Area
■	Building
—·—·—	Forest or Wilderness Area Boundary
≈≈	Glacier
▲	Mountain
○	Town

The Pacific Crest Trail

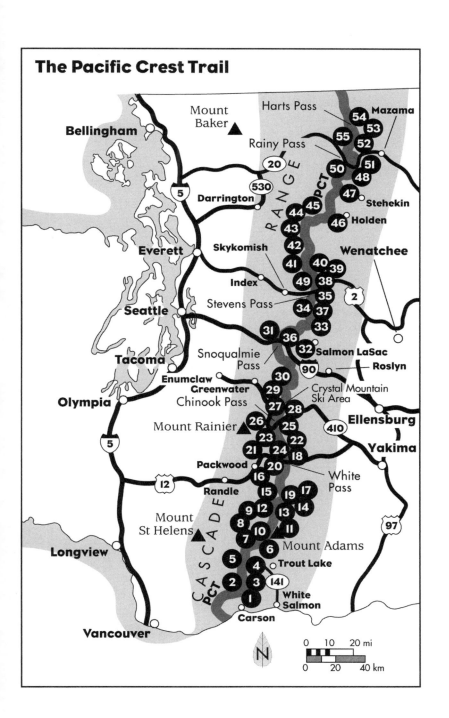

PREFACE

The Pacific Crest National Scenic Trail is one of the crown jewels in the National Trail System, but it is seldom enjoyed to its fullest by the hikers who live nearest to it. Why? Because the 2,650-mile trail is daunting in its size. In Washington alone, the Pacific Crest Trail (PCT) extends some 500 miles from the Bridge of the Gods over the Columbia River to Monument 78 at the Canadian Border. This is an impressive number of trail miles, surely, but most hiking on the PCT is restricted to the few miles on either side of the primary highway passes over the Cascades: White Pass (US 12), Chinook Pass (SR 410), Snoqualmie Pass (I-90), Stevens Pass (US 2), and Rainy Pass (SR 20—the North Cascades Highway). If day hikers hike 5 miles north and south from these passes, they cover just 10 percent of the PCT in Washington. Although many of the sections near the passes are stunning, the rest of the "best" of the PCT is found well beyond these easy-access sections.

THE HISTORY

The Pacific Crest Trails Association reports that the concept of a high route from border to border was first publicly discussed by a Bellingham author, Joseph T. Hazard, in 1926. The idea was already being developed as early as 1920, however, when the rangers from Region 6 (Washington and Oregon) of the U.S. Forest Service (USFS) began construction of the Skyline Trail in Oregon. This trail stretched along the Cascade Crest from Mount Hood to Crater Lake. When Fred Cleator was appointed recreation supervisor for Region 6 in 1928, he immediately set about creating a trail from Canada to the Columbia River, naming it the Cascade Crest Trail. These two trails formed the backbone of the Pacific Crest Trail System by the early 1930s.

In 1932, Clinton C. Clarke of Pasadena, California, began writing letters to the USFS, the National Park Service, and members of Congress, advocating the creation of a crest trail. He soon took the idea public and drafted the members of the Mountain League of Los Angeles to help promote the trail idea. He encouraged other clubs to join the effort and in late 1932, Clark founded the Pacific Crest Trail System Conference. Members of this new coalition included the Boy Scouts of America, the Sierra Club, the Mazamas of Oregon, and The Mountaineers among others. The trail managers for USFS Region 6, led by Cleator, quickly developed a new emblem for the trail. Trail markers bearing a white-and-green diamond, embossed with the words *Pacific Crest Trail System* around a tall evergreen were posted along the Skyline Trail and the Cascade Crest Trail. These markers can still be found today along sections of the trail, particularly between Naches Pass and the Indian Heaven Wilderness Area.

Between 1932 and the early 1960s, the PCT was discussed, mapped, and largely ignored by all but a handful of enthusiasts. But in the 1960s, hiking boomed in popularity. The Appalachian Trail was complete, and its proponents were demanding national recognition and protection for the 2,000-mile trail. Meanwhile, environmental issues, including wildlands protection, were becoming national issues. In 1965, President Lyndon Johnson called for the creation of a national system of trails. A multi-agency commission studied trails nationwide and published a report, "Trails for America," in 1966. This report identified four types of trails needing protection: scenic trails in wilderness-like settings, recreation trails around more developed areas, historic trails along routes of national historic importance, and connecting trails accessing the other trails.

"Trails for America" was used to create the National Trails System Act, passed by Congress and signed into law in 1968. Under this act, the Appalachian Trail and the Pacific Crest Trail were named the first two National Scenic Trails. Since then, the Pacific Crest Trail has been mapped, rerouted, and built. The trail was dedicated thirty years after its formal birth, with a "Gold Spike" completion ceremony held on National Trails Day, 1998.

All 2,650 miles of the Pacific Crest Trail are now reality (though some 300 of them are on narrow, unprotected easements along public highways and across private lands). Relatively few of us will ever enjoy all those miles, but we all benefit from the trail's existence. We don't need to spend months slogging single-mindedly up the trail to experience the PCT. Indeed, the trail can be enjoyed by all hikers, whether out for a few hours or a few days.

The motivation behind writing this book was to encourage hikers to enjoy the PCT in realistic portions. Existing guidebooks for the PCT focus on mile-by-mile descriptions of the entire border-to-border trail as it rolls north from Mexico to Canada. These books are ideal for hikers who plan to spend weeks, or months, hiking significant portions of the trail. Yet, those long-distance hikers comprise only a tiny percentage of the entire hiking population. The rest of us tend to spend most of our trail time on day outings or backpacking trips of no more than 3 or 4 days.

Because little information is available about how to enjoy the immense PCT in short periods of time, vast sections of the trail are ignored by the majority of the hiking community.

Best of the Pacific Crest Trail: Washington aims to provide you, the average hiker, with the information you need to enjoy the beauty of this wonderful trail in whatever time is available to you, whether it's a week, a long weekend, or just a day.

THE FUTURE

A guidebook does no good if the trails it describes disappear. Lack of funding for routine maintenance has led to a serious problem of neglect on much of the PCT. Congress created the trail in 1968, but in the intervening thirty years, lawmakers haven't provided the funding needed for basic annual maintenance, let alone for projects such as trail relocation, bridge reconstruction, and long-term erosion control measures. Where Congress has failed, though, volunteers have succeeded.

In 1987, the Pacific Crest Trail Association (PCTA), a reorganization and expansion of the original Pacific Crest Trail System Conference, signed a Memorandum of Understanding with the USDA Forest Service to help maintain and promote the trail through Adopt-A-Trail and other volunteer efforts. The PCTA advocates for greater protection of the trail, especially in those areas where the trail is threatened by development and commercial activities, and publishes a bimonthly magazine.

In the early 1990s, the Washington Trails Association (WTA) recognized a significant lack of routine maintenance on most of the state's backcountry trails, including the PCT. To address the need, WTA created a volunteer trail maintenance program that, in less than five years, was so successful it was performing up to 75 percent of the annual maintenance hours spent on trails in the Mount Baker–Snoqualmie National Forest.

WTA now coordinates more than 300 days—over 50,000 total hours—of volunteer trail maintenance annually, and nearly a quarter of that is devoted to the PCT and its network of side access trails. Volunteers can work a single day, or join weeklong work parties that WTA leads into the backcountry. In 1999, WTA hosted nineteen weeklong work parties, and more than a third of them were located somewhere along the PCT.

The WTA Trail Maintenance Program has helped prevent the loss of thousands of miles of trail to simple neglect, but if the program is to continue to be successful, WTA needs new participants. Even though the program has a very high rate of return among first-timers, new volunteers are always needed to keep the teams energized and effective. If you enjoy hiking in Washington, consider spending at least one day a year on a trail maintenance project.

Not only is volunteering for trail work a very rewarding experience in and of itself, but it has an added bonus in these days of high recreational user fees. For every day you spend on a volunteer work party (on USFS lands), you will receive one Day Trail Park Pass. When you've earned two Day Trail Park Passes, you can trade them in for an Annual Trail Park Pass.

Old, original PCT emblems can be found along the remains of the old Cascade Crest Trail.

You don't need to worry about work experience, either. No prior trail maintenance experience is necessary, and WTA has volunteers of all ages and physical abilities. WTA spends most of its time on the trails attending to annual maintenance tasks, such as brushing and lopping to remove plants or tree limbs that are encroaching on the trailway. Volunteers also play in the dirt, repairing tread in places where it has been destroyed by slides, or washouts. And for those who never outgrew their childhood delight in playing in the mud, volunteers also muck out mud-clogged ditches, drain-dips, and culverts to make sure they are carrying water effectively. WTA provides all the tools and training necessary for each work project, asking only that you wear the appropriate clothing and bring a lunch, water, and a desire to have fun while getting some important work done.

If you find you enjoy hiking on any of the trails listed in this guidebook, please set aside at least one day in your schedule to help keep the trails safe and open. If we all do this, we can guarantee that the 500 miles of the PCT in Washington state will continue to exist despite the lack of support from the politicians in the "other" Washington.

To receive information on WTA Trail Teams, contact WTA's Director of Operations, 1305 Fourth Avenue, Suite 512, Seattle, WA 98101; (206) 625-1367; or visit *www.wta.org*. To receive information about the Pacific Crest Trail Association, write to the PCTA, 5325 Elkhorn Blvd. PMB 256, Sacramento, CA 95842; call toll-free (888) PCTRAIL [728-7245]; or visit *www.pcta.org*.

A NOTE ABOUT SAFETY

Safety is an important concern in all outdoor activities. No guidebook can alert you to every hazard or anticipate the limitations of every reader. Therefore, the descriptions of roads, trails, routes, and natural features in this book are not representations that a particular place or excursion will be safe for your party. When you follow any of the routes described in this book, you assume responsibility for your own safety. Under normal conditions, such excursions require the usual attention to traffic, road and trail conditions, weather, terrain, the capabilities of your party, and other factors. Keeping informed on current conditions and exercising common sense are the keys to a safe, enjoyable outing.

—*The Mountaineers*

INTRODUCTION

From the Columbia River to the Canadian Border, the Pacific Crest Trail (PCT) serpentines north across nine wilderness areas and four national forests and then dips into two national parks, a national recreation area, and a national scenic area. State and private lands also shelter parts of the trail.

For 500 miles the trail crawls north across the spine of the Cascades, offering some of the most rugged, remote hiking in the country. There are sections that can be seen only by making a long 3-day hike, and others that cross pristine wilderness that hasn't changed since Lewis and Clark found passage through the Columbia River Gorge.

Hiking in the Cascades is one of the most enjoyable pursuits you'll ever experience, but it can also be one of the most deadly. All that beautiful, natural wilderness poses great danger to ill-prepared and unsuspecting hikers. A stroll through a sunny wildflower meadow at 6,000 feet in the North Cascades can become a nightmare struggle through a slippery, sodden field of mud in a matter of moments. Thunderstorms can develop and blow in with little or no advance warning.

A day hike can turn into a rescue operation if you happen to twist an ankle while crossing a talus slope and end up having to spend the night waiting while someone else makes the long hike out, summons medical personnel, and then leads them back to you. The key to having an enjoyable and safe hike is in being prepared, not just for the conditions you expect to encounter but for the unexpected ones as well.

PERMITS AND REGULATIONS

You can't set off out your door these days without first making sure you're not breaking any rules. In an effort to keep our wilderness areas wild and our trails safe and well-maintained, land managers—especially the National Park Service and the USFS—have implemented a sometimes-complex set of rules and regulations governing the use of public lands.

Fortunately, the rules governing the PCT are fairly straightforward and fair. First off, the PCT is open to hikers and horse riders only. No motorized vehicles of any kind, and no bicycles, are allowed on the trail.

View down to Sheep Lake from Sourdough Gap

The sections of the trail within any national forests in Washington fall under the Region 6 Trail Park Pass Program. Simply stated, in order to park legally at any national forest trailhead in USFS Region 6 (Washington and Oregon), you must display a Region 6 Trail Park Pass decal in your windshield. These sell for $3 per day or $25 for an annual pass, which is good throughout Region 6.

When the trail enters a wilderness area, you must pick up and fill out a wilderness permit at the trailhead registration box (sometimes located at the wilderness boundary if the trail doesn't immediately enter a designated wilderness). For the time being, these permits are free and unlimited (at least on the trailheads covered in this book).

Because the PCT just grazes Mount Rainier National Park, its strict backcountry camping regulations supersede those of the PCT; North Cascades National Park has never had any wilderness restrictions.

View of Mount Rainier from the PCT above Crystal Mountain resort

LOW-IMPACT CAMPING

We all love to sit around a campfire, letting the orange flames hypnotize us and stir up a wealth of thoughts and dreams. Unfortunately, if we all built fires in wilderness settings, the campsites would be filled with charcoal and the forests would soon be picked clean of dead wood, leaving the hordes of small critters who depend on it with nowhere to scrounge for food. (The insects that eat dead wood provide meals for an army of birds and animals.) So leave fires to the car campgrounds with their structured fire pits and readily available supplies of firewood. If you want to camp responsibly in the backcountry, stick to a small pack stove, even when regulations technically allow campfires.

You must also remember that anything that is packed in must be packed out, even biodegradable items like apple cores. The phrase "leave only footprints, take only pictures" is a worthy slogan to live by when visiting the wilderness.

You must also give some thought to your campsites. When hardened sites are available, use them. The practice of restricting campers to one or two sites around a lake prevents the entire shoreline from being trampled and stripped of its vegetation. If there is no established site, choose a rocky or sandy area where you won't damage fragile vegetation. If you must camp in a meadow area, choose a location with good drainage and restrict the time that your tent is set up. Rather than pitch the tent immediately upon reaching your camp, leave it in its stuff sack until you are done with dinner, and then set it up. First thing next morning, break it down before breakfast—this prevents the plants underneath the tent from being smothered, and most of the time, even though they are a bit bent and crumpled, they'll spring back up again soon.

Also keep in mind that you aren't the only hikers out enjoying the beauty of the wilderness. That rocky bench overlooking the mountains across the valley might seem like the perfect place for a tent, but what if you set up there and someone else comes along behind and wants to just sit and enjoy the view for a few moments? With your camp established on the viewpoint, other hikers will feel uncomfortable stepping up for a look out at the vista. It's a much better idea to set up well back from the most scenic locations so that you can still walk to them from camp and enjoy them, but so can the other hikers who share the trail with you.

The same courtesy applies to the wilderness water supply. Keep your camp at least 100 feet away from lakeshores and streambanks. This not

What not *to do: These campers have set up too close to the lake and also block other hikers' view of the scenery.*

only lets other hikers—and animals—get to the water without having to bypass you, but it helps to keep the water clean.

Another important "Leave No Trace" principle focuses on the matter of taking care of personal business. The first rule of backcountry bathroom etiquette says that if an outhouse exists, use it. This seems obvious, but all too often, folks find backcountry toilets are dark, dank affairs and they choose to use the woods rather than the rickety wooden structure provided by the land manager. It may be easier on your nose to head off into the woods, but this disperses human waste all around the popular camping areas. Privies, on the other hand, keep the waste concentrated in a single site, minimizing contamination of area waters. The outhouses get even higher environmental marks if they feature removable holding tanks that can be airlifted out. These johns and their accompanying stack of tanks aren't exactly aesthetically pleasing, but it's better than finding toilet paper strewn throughout the woods.

When privies aren't provided, the key factor to consider is location. You'll want to choose a site at least 200 to 300 feet from water, campsites, and trails. A location well out of sight of trails and viewpoints will give you privacy and reduce the odds of other hikers stumbling upon the site after you leave. Other factors to consider are ecological: a good surrounding of vegetation, with some direct sunlight, will aid decomposition.

Once you pick your place, start digging. The idea is to make like a cat and bury your waste, but not your toilet paper. You must pack out the paper. Dig down through the organic duff into the mineral soil below—a hole six to eight inches deep is usually adequate. When you've taken care of business, refill the hole and camouflage it with rocks and sticks—this helps prevent other humans, or animals, from digging in the same location before decomposition has done its job.

WATER

You must treat your drinking water. Wherever humans have gone, germs have gone with them, and humans have gone just about everywhere. This means that even the most pristine mountain stream may harbor microscopic nasties like giardia cysts, cryptosporidium, or E. coli.

Treating water can be as simple as boiling it, chemically purifying it (by adding tiny iodine tablets), or pumping it through one of the new generation water filters or purifiers. Pump units labeled as filters generally remove everything but viruses, which are too small to be filtered out. Pumps labeled as purifiers use a chemical element—usually iodine—that kills the viruses after filtering out all the other bugs. Remember, don't drink untreated water, or your intestines will never forgive you.

CLEAN-UP

When it comes time to wash up, whether it's just your hands or your dinner pots, give some thought to the quality of the water that you drink. You get your drinking water from the nearby lake or stream, right? Would you want to find someone's leftover macaroni and cheese in it? Or their soap scum? Of course not, and neither would they, so be careful with your clean-ups.

When washing your hands, rinse off as much dust and dirt as you can using plain water first. If you still feel the need for a soapy wash, collect a pot of water from the lake or stream and move at least 100 feet away. Apply a tiny bit of biodegradable soap to your hands, dribble on a little water, and lather up. Use a bandanna or towel to wipe away most of the soap, then rinse with the water in the pot. Follow the same procedure with your pots and pans, making sure you've eaten all the food first. (Never dump leftover food in the water or on the ground. If you can't eat it, pack it in a plastic bag and store it with your other food—in other words, carry it out!)

BEARS

Speaking of food, you need to follow the proper method for bear-bagging your food and heavily scented clothing items (i.e., shirts with lots of sweat and/or deodorant). There are an estimated 30,000 to 35,000 black bears in Washington, and the big bruins can be found in every corner of the state. The high, wild country around the PCT is especially attractive to the solitude-seeking bears, and they can be found roaming every inch of the PCT in Washington. Watching bears graze through a rich huckleberry patch or seeing them flip dead logs in search of grubs can be an exciting and rewarding experience. Provided, of course, you aren't in the same berry patch. Bears tend to prefer solitude to human company, and they will generally flee long before you have a chance to get too close. There are times, however, when bears either don't hear hikers approaching or they are more interested in defending their food source—or their young— than they are in avoiding a confrontation. These instances are rare, and you can further minimize the odds of an encounter with an aggressive bear by taking the following precautions:

◆ Hike in a group and hike only during daylight hours.

◆ Talk or sing as you hike. If a bear hears you coming, it will usually avoid you. On the other hand, a bear feels threatened when it is surprised, and often goes on the offensive in a surprise encounter, at least until it feels the threat is neutralized. So make noises that will identify you as a human—talk, sing, rattle pebbles in a tin can—especially when hiking near a river or stream (which can mask more subtle sounds that might normally alert a bear to your presence).

◆ Be aware of the environment around you, and know how to identify "bear sign." Overturned rocks and torn-up logs are often the result of a bear searching for grubs. Berry bushes stripped of berries, with leaves, branches, and berries littering the ground under the bushes, show where a bear has fed. Bears will often leave claw marks on trees and, because they use trees as scratch-ing posts, fur in the rough bark says, "A bear was here!" Tracks and scat are the most common signs of a bear's recent presence.

◆ Stay away from abundant food sources and dead animals. Black bears are opportunistic and will scavenge food. A bear that finds a dead deer will hang around until the meat is gone, and it will defend that food against any perceived threat.

◆ Keep dogs on leash and under control. Many bear encounters

The Pacific Crest Trail near Cutthroat Pass

have resulted from unleashed dogs chasing a bear. When the bear gets angry and turns on the dog, the dog gets scared and runs for help (i.e., back to its owner), and the bear follows it right back into the dog owner's lap.

◆ Leave perfume, hairspray, cologne, and scented soaps at home. Using scented sprays and body lotions makes you smell like a big, tasty treat.

Unfortunately, not all hikers behave as they should in bear country. Bears are intelligent animals and opportunistic feeders—they will seek out easy meals wherever they can. That's why some bears have learned that sloppy hikers can provide good, tasty meals. These bears have learned to watch human camps and look for the slobs among us. To avoid being targeted as a "sloppy hiker," take the following measures:

◆ Never eat or cook in your tent. Spilled food or even food odors can permeate the nylon material, essentially making your tent smell, at least to a bear, like last night's dinner.

◆ Always clean fish at least 100 feet away from camp—200 feet is even better!

◆ Always store all your food and other scented items in their own stuff sacks when preparing to hang them. (In other words, don't use your sleeping bag's stuff sack or the food odors can be transferred to the sack and then to the sleeping bag, making the bear think you are a big, smelly meatroll.)

◆ Always suspend your food bags at least 12 feet in the air and 8 to 10 feet from the nearest tree trunk. In some popular backcountry camps, the land managers provide wires, complete with pulleys, to help you do this, but you'll need to know how to string your own rope to achieve these heights, too.

◆ Never try to lure wild animals with food. One notable case in Washington's Olympic National Park comes to mind. A young couple wanted to have the local chipmunks come closer to their tent so they could get pictures, so they laid down a line of chocolate candies from a jumble of nearby logs to their tent entrance. They then ducked into the tent with camera at the ready. Soon they heard something moving outside, snuffling up the candy. Expecting a cute little squirrel, they got a chocolate-happy black bear. Their yells scared the bear away, but the situation could have turned out differently.

On the very rare occasion, hikers can do all the right things and a bear will still behave aggressively. It could be as simple as being in the wrong place at the wrong time—I once found myself between a black bear sow and one of her cubs simply because the cub had wandered downhill of the trail while the sow was uphill of it. Fortunately, youngster was a second-year cub and momma bear was ready to toss it out on its own at any time, so she barely looked up from her huckleberry dinner as I grouped the hikers behind me into a tight cluster and hustled everyone up the trail. But the bear could have turned aggressive. If you find yourself in that situation, here are some guidelines to follow in an encounter:

- ◆ Respect a bear's need for personal space. If you see a bear in the distance, make a wide detour around it, or if that's not possible (i.e., if the trail leads close to the bear) leave the area.
- ◆ If you encounter a bear at close range, remain calm. Do not run because this could trigger a predator/prey reaction from the bear.
- ◆ Talk to the bear in a calm manner with a low voice to help identify yourself as a human.
- ◆ Hold your arms out from your body, and if wearing a jacket, hold open the front so you appear to be as big as possible.
- ◆ Don't stare directly at the bear—the bear may interpret this as a direct threat or challenge. Watch the animal without making direct eye-to-eye contact.
- ◆ Slowly move upwind of the bear if you can do so without crowding the bear. The bear's keenest sense is its sense of smell, and if it can sniff you and identify you as human, it may retreat.
- ◆ Know how to interpret bear actions. A nervous bear will often rumble in its chest, clack its teeth, and "pop" its jaw. It may paw the ground and swing its head violently side to side. If the bear does this, watch it closely (without staring directly at it). Continue to speak calmly in a low voice.
- ◆ A bear may bluff-charge—run at you but stop well before reaching you—to try and intimidate you. Resist the urge to run from this charge because that would turn the bluff into a real charge, and you will NOT be able to outrun the bear. (Black bears can run at speeds up to 35 miles per hour through log-strewn forests.)
- ◆ If you surprise a bear and it charges from close range, lie down and play dead. A surprised bear will leave you once the perceived threat is neutralized. However, if the bear wasn't attacking

because it was surprised—if it charges from a long distance, or if it has had a chance to identify you and still attacks—you should fight back. A bear in this situation is behaving in a predatory manner (as opposed to the defensive attack of a surprised bear), and it is looking at you as food. Kick, stab, and punch at the bear. If it knows you will fight back, it may leave you and search for easier prey.

◆ Carry a 12-ounce (or larger) can of pepper-spray bear deterrent. The spray—a high concentration of oils from hot peppers—should fire out at least 20 or 30 feet in a broad mist. Don't use the spray unless a bear is actually charging and is within range of the spray.

COUGARS

Very few hikers ever see cougars in the wild. Not only are these big cats solitary, shy animals of the woods, but there are just 2,500 to 3,000 of them roaming the entire state of Washington. Still, cougars and hikers do sometimes encounter each other. If you find yourself in this situation, in my opinion, you should count your blessings—you will likely never see a more majestic animal than a wild cougar. To make sure the encounter is a positive one, you must understand the cats. Cougars are shy but very curious. They will follow you simply to see what kind of beast you are, but they very rarely (as in almost never) attack adult humans. If you do encounter a cougar, remember that cougars rely on prey that can't, or won't, fight back. So as soon as you see the cat, follow these steps:

◆ Do not run! Running may trigger a cougar's attack instinct.
◆ Stand up and face the animal. Virtually every recorded cougar attack of humans has been a predator/prey attack. If you appear as another aggressive predator rather than as prey, the cougar will back down.
◆ Try to appear large—wave your arms or a jacket over your head. The idea is to make the cougar think you are the bigger, meaner beast.
◆ Pick up children.
◆ Maintain eye contact with the animal. The cougar will interpret this as a show of dominance on your part.
◆ Do not approach the animal; back away slowly if you can safely do so.

Exploration off-trail near Glacier Peak reveals lots of ice-cold creeks in deep granite valleys.

The cougar may not find you convincing as a threat, and it may continue to display aggressive behavior, especially toward women and teens (i.e., people with smaller body frames). If this is the case, follow these steps:

◆ Do not turn your back on or take your eyes off the cougar.

◆ Remain standing.

◆ Throw objects, provided you don't have to bend over to pick them up. If you have a water bottle on your belt, chuck it at the cat. Throw your camera, wave your hiking stick, and if the cat gets close enough, whack it HARD with your hiking staff. (I know of two cases in which women delivered good, hard whacks across the nose of aggressive-acting cougars, and the cats immediately turned tail and ran away.)

◆ Shout loudly.

◆ Fight back aggressively.

You can minimize the already slim chances of having a negative cougar encounter by doing the following:

◆ Do not hike or jog alone. (In fact, don't jog at all—joggers look like fleeing prey to a predator.)

◆ Keep children within sight and close at all times.

◆ Avoid dead animals.

◆ Keep a clean camp.

◆ Keep dogs on leash and under control. A cougar may attack a loose, solitary dog, but a leashed dog next to you makes two foes for the cougar to deal with—and cougars are too smart to take on two aggressive animals at once.

◆ Be alert to the surroundings.

◆ Use a walking stick.

Remember, above all else, cougars are curious animals. They may appear threatening when they are only being inquisitive. By making the cougar think you are a bigger, meaner critter than it is, you will be able to avoid an attack. (The big cats recognize that enough easy prey exists so that they don't have to mess with something that fights back.) Keep in mind that fewer than twenty fatal cougar attacks have occurred in the United States in the past 100 years. (On the other hand, more than fifty people are killed, on average, by deer each year—most in auto collisions with the deer.)

WEATHER

Wild weather is a far greater threat to PCT hikers than wild animals. The trail runs through some of the most remote high country in the state. Mountain weather in general is famously unpredictable, but the Cascade Mountains stretch that unpredictability to sometimes-absurd lengths. The high, jagged nature of the mountains, coupled with their proximity to the Pacific Ocean, makes them magnets for every bit of moisture in the atmosphere.

As moist air comes rushing in off the Pacific, it hits the western front of the Cascades. The air is then pushed up the slopes of the mountains, forming clouds and eventually rain that feeds the rain forests that dominate the western slopes. By the time the air stream crests the Cascades and starts down the eastern slopes, the clouds have lost their moisture loads, leaving the east side dry. As a result, eastern forests are made up of open stands of drought-resistant pine.

Where east meets west—roughly marked by the Pacific Crest Trail— the wet clouds hit the dry heat, often creating thunderstorms. You must be aware of this potential when you're on the trail because storms can brew up during any month of the year. They can also come up quickly and with little warning. If you're hiking on a high pass when a thunderstorm is developing, you've just become a prime target for a lightning bolt.

To reduce the danger of being struck by lightning if thunderstorms are forecast or they develop while you are in the mountains, take the following precautions:

◆ Use a NOAA weather radio (i.e., a radio set to tune in to one of the national weather forecast frequencies) to keep abreast of the latest weather information.

Near Mica Lake, one hiker zips up to block out the weather.

- ◆ Avoid travel on mountaintops and ridge crests.
- ◆ Avoid setting up camp in narrow valleys or gullies, or on ridge tops. Instead, look for campsites in broad, open valleys and meadows, keeping away from large rock formations.
- ◆ Stay well away from bodies of water.
- ◆ If your hair stands on end or you feel static shocks, move immediately—the static electricity you feel could very well be a precursor to a lightning strike.
- ◆ If a shelter or building is nearby, get into it. Don't take shelter under trees, however, especially in open areas.
- ◆ If no shelter is available and lightning is flashing, remove your pack (the metal stays or frame are natural electrical conduits) and crouch down, balancing on the balls of your feet until the lightning clears the area.

Of course, thunderstorms aren't the only weather hazard you might face on the PCT. A sudden rainsquall can push temperatures down 15 or 20 degrees in a matter of minutes. If you're dressed for hot summer hiking, you also need to be prepared for sudden drops in temperature, and the accompanying soaking rain, in order to avoid hypothermia.

If the temperature drop is great enough, you can end up missing the rain and getting hit instead by snow. I've seen snowstorms blow through the Cascades every month of the year, with as much as a foot falling on some routes in late August.

Besides fresh-fallen snow, summer hikers need to be aware of snowfields left over from the previous winter's snowpack. Depending on the severity of the past winter, and the weather conditions of the spring and early summer, parts of the PCT may melt out in June while other parts remain snow-covered well into August or beyond. In some years, certain sections never melt out.

In addition to presenting you with treacherous footing and difficulties in routefinding, these lingering snowfields can be prone to avalanches or slides.

TRAIL CONDITIONS AND DANGERS

The PCT suffers from the problems of other mountain trails, but it has problems all its own, too. Because the trail is one of the highest in the Cascades and long sections of it traverse the most remote country in the state, there are particular difficulties in keeping the trail maintained.

The first problem you will encounter is snow. Rolling around the flanks of the great Cascade volcanoes and over the jagged ridges of the lesser—but no less rugged—peaks, the PCT accumulates deep snow in the winter. And that snow is typically slow to melt in the spring and summer—so slow that the PCT (especially the northern section) is often one of the last trails in the state to open. You should always be prepared for snowy conditions, even in summer. Sturdy hiking boots and gaiters are required, and trekking poles are advised.

Lingering snow also poses problems for the maintenance crews who take care of the trails. The workers can't get in to clear and maintain the trails until the snow melts, and when substantial work needs to be done, a late melt-out can prevent the work from being completed. The more remote sections of the PCT are often littered with fallen trees and may have structural damage, ranging from washed-out sections to missing bridges.

Missing bridges can be especially dangerous. When a bridge is out, you typically have to ford the stream, and while a river may look mild-mannered and easy to cross, hidden dangers lurk under the surface. If you are an inexperienced wader, you might be surprised by the pressure that is exerted by even a slow-moving stream. The water seems to try to push your feet out from under you, while the slime-covered rocks that line the riverbed aid that effort by preventing you from finding firm footing. Also, mountain streams are fed by the melting snow, and they can be nearly as cold as the snow itself. It takes only a few steps into a snow-melt creek before your feet are numb with cold, further reducing your ability to find good footing.

When you do get across, remember that conditions can change rapidly in the mountains. If you head up a trail in

This Bullion Basin trailhead sign banning motorcycles has been knocked down and run over.

the morning, the snow is still solid after the typically cool night. But as the sun climbs in the sky and the air warms, the snow starts to melt again. As it does, the water swells the streams below. That means the quiet, calm creek you crossed early in the day could be a raging torrent by the time you return in the evening. More hikers fall during evening fords rather than morning fords simply because the higher water, combined with the fact they are tired after a day-long trek, makes them more prone to accidents while wading.

Another problem you might face on the PCT is downed trees. Again, because work crews can't get in and clear the trail until the snow melts, it's sometimes September or later before work can be scheduled for the more remote sections of the crest trail. That means you may have to scramble over, under, or around blown-down trees. Barkless trees are dangerous because their smooth skin can be very slippery; dead trees that fall over the trail often have short, sharp branch spurs protruding out like spines on a porcupine. You need to be careful when crossing these trees so you don't slip and skewer yourself on one of the spearlike branches.

GEAR

FOOTWEAR

No hiker should venture far up a trail without being properly equipped. Starting with the feet, a good pair of boots can make the difference between a wonderful hike and a horrible death march. Keep your feet happy and you'll be happy.

Taking care of your feet before, during, and after a hike is the key to enjoyable outings on the trails. That being the case, it's amazing how many hikers don't take the time to make sure that their feet are fit. Strong, well-cared-for feet come from having a system of footwear that not only fits well but performs well.

To get the best boot and sock, you need to start with your bare feet. Measure your feet—not just length and width but general foot volume, too—and then look for a pair of boots in the correct size and in a style that matches the requirements of the terrain in which you'll be hiking.

Where and how you'll be hiking should have a big impact on the kind of boots you purchase. Heavier, full-grain leather boots are generally the most supportive and durable; those are an excellent choice for hearty backpacking adventures. Uppers (i.e., the part of the boot above the sole) made with a combination of fabric and leather will breathe a little better and are lighter, so they are best worn on day hikes and overnight trips with light packs when you'll be staying on a trail.

When buying boots, plan on spending a couple of hours doing it. Head for the store in the afternoon, after you've been up and moving around for a few hours at least so that your feet are swollen to their normal "use" size. When you get to the store, head straight for the boot department. If you have other shopping to do, you can do it while wear-testing the boots you're considering.

The first thing to do when you get the box of boots you'll be trying on is to yank out the flimsy foam insoles that come standard in today's hiking boots. These are totally worthless bits of fluff—they provide no structure or support, and after an hour or two of use, no padding. An insole should stabilize and support your foot to prevent over-pronation (carrying your weight on the outside of your foot as you stride), a condition experienced by more than 80 percent of the population. A good third-party insole will cost $25 to $65 depending on whether you go for an over-the-counter pre-made version or a custom-fit model.

After replacing the insole, try on the boots and examine the fit, not only for length and width but also for volume. If the boots have too much volume, your feet will slide forward, which crumples your toes into the boot end and allows your heels to slide around, generating blisters. You want room for your toes to move comfortably, but your heel should be secure and there shouldn't be excess material around your ankle or arch.

To check the volume, lace the boots up nice and snug. Next, stand on an incline board, pointing your toes uphill, and have the sales clerk or a friend wrap their hand around the top of your forefoot right over the laces with fingers and thumb pointing back toward the heel. As they squeeze down around your foot and ankle, have them look for loose material under their fingers and the ball of their thumb. If there is loose material, that shows there is too much volume in the boots and you'll slide around in them. Many hiking boot manufacturers err toward higher volume boots, so you could discover a problem.

But there are ways to compensate. Use of a "tongue-depressor," or a wedge of dense foam, slipped between the laces and boot tongue will take up a lot of that volume, as will thick, dense socks.

Speaking of socks, bear in mind that there's a lot more going on your feet than just boots. Wearing the right socks is equally as important as getting the correct boots. When you shop for new boots, of course take along a pair of your favorite hiking socks, but also be prepared to try on (and buy!) different socks, because the socks you normally wear might not be the best match for the boots you're buying (or, for that matter, for your feet). Technical hiking socks come in a dizzying array of shapes and fabric blends. Remember, though, that socks have a few specific job requirements: they should cushion the transition from your feet to your boots, move moisture away from your skin, insulate your feet in cool climates, and fill in the "voids" in high-volume boots.

Socks also protect your feet from themselves. When selecting socks, the main point to keep in mind is sweat. Your feet will sweat.

With that in mind, never wear cotton for anything more active than walking from your office cubicle to the water cooler. Cotton feels great, until you start to sweat. Then cotton grabs onto that moisture and traps it right against your skin. Your skin softens, and any friction (as from walking) will cause a blister. The only cotton that goes into the backcountry with me is my pink, cotton bandanna—pink because nobody else I know would be caught dead carrying a pink bandanna, so I always know which one is mine!

The other natural fiber, wool—especially the soft merino wool used in many technical garments today—is a much better sock material. Wool is a good insulator, and it does pull moisture away from the skin. But if you sweat extensively, steer clear of wool, at least in the warmer months, because unlike some of the technical synthetic fabrics, wool doesn't transport moisture to the outside of the sock—it merely absorbs it. Although wool can absorb a lot of water, it does reach a saturation point, and then it's like wearing a waterlogged sponge in your boot.

Speaking of synthetic socks, look for socks that utilize a hydrophobic (moisture repelling) material. As you sweat, the pressure of walking will push the sweat through the sock and the hydrophobic nature of the material will spread the moisture across the top of your foot where it can "breathe" out through the boot's upper. An even better bet is to go for a dual-layer sock that puts a hydrophobic fabric on the bottom of the sock and a hydrophilic (or moisture-attracting) fabric on the top. This creates a push-pull action to really get the water away from your skin.

With your socks, insoles, and boots in hand, you're ready to hike—almost. Even though many boot makers today claim their boots don't require a break-in period, plan to wear them around the house or on walks in your neighborhood for a week or two before your first hike. The flex-points in the boots need to loosen up so they "break" with your foot. Your new insoles also need some time to mold and conform to your feet, just as you'll need some time to get accustomed to your new insoles. It's better to walk out any kinks and find any problems in your own backyard than out in the wild Cascades.

SLEEPING BAGS

A good, three-season tent for shelter and a fluffy, lightweight sleeping bag—with a small pad (used as much for insulation from the cold ground as padding)—are the primary items in your pack.

Selecting a sleeping bag can be difficult, if only because the selection of bags from which to choose has gotten so large. Let's start with the shape of the bag. The tapered, body-hugging shape of a mummy bag eliminates extra fabric and insulation—and therefore extra weight—while creating an efficient insulation cocoon. The tapered shape means there is less area inside the bag for your body to heat up, so less energy is expended as you sleep.

Some people, however, feel like a trussed-up turkey in mummy bags. If you're one of them, a semi-rectangular cut can be a good compromise. The bag is tapered, but dramatically less so than most mummies. The tradeoff is that the bag weighs a bit more, but it is less confining so you'll sleep better.

After you settle on the general shape of your bag, you need to consider where and when you'll be using it. Specifically, you need to consider how warm you want the bag to be. Sleeping-bag makers classify their products according to temperature ratings—an indication of the minimal outside temperature at which the bag will be comfortable. But these ratings aren't standardized, and they are meant to serve as general guidelines for the average person. When you shop for a bag, consider your normal sleeping conditions and whether you are a warm sleeper or a cold sleeper.

For most three-season hiking, a bag rated to 15° F or 20° F is ideal. If you'll be camping only in the summer months, you might get by with a 40° F or 50° F bag. If you plan to camp in winter, you'll want a bag rated to 0° F or even –10° F—depending on where you'll be doing your winter camping. Mountaineers and snow hikers in the far northern latitudes often opt for a bag rated to –30° F.

The insulation value of a bag depends mostly on the type of insulation used. There are two classifications of insulation in sleeping bags—down and synthetic. Down is lighter and compacts more (i.e., stuffs smaller) than any of the synthetics, but it loses all its insulation properties when it gets wet (keep that in mind if you plan to be hiking in humid or rainy areas). Down is coded with a fill number. The higher the number, the more compactible it is and the better its insulation value. For example, 700-fill down is lighter and compacts more than 550-fill down.

There are scores of synthetic fill materials in use, but only a handful are useful in backpacking sleeping bags. These all share common traits; most notably they are compactible and durable. When deciding on down or synthetic, bear in mind that although down is lighter and more stuffable than any of the synthetic fills, the synthetics have two points in their favor. First, synthetic fill bags are much less expensive, on average, than similar down bags. Second, synthetic fills hold their ability to insulate even when wet—a definite plus when hiking in wet regions such as the Pacific Northwest.

Your selection criteria should also evaluate the assortment of features offered in the bag. A good backcountry bag will have an insulated draft collar. This is an insulated tube sewn around the neck or upper chest area of the bag. It can usually be drawn tight via a cinch strap to seal out any cold air that might leak in around your head. A hood is also an important feature. This extended portion of the bag fits up around the back of your head and can be cinched shut so that only your nose and mouth are exposed during the coldest nights.

An insulated zipper draft tube is a good feature to look for if you want to thoroughly seal in your warmth. This bag-length tube runs behind the closed zipper and insulates against air drafts.

Secondary features to consider are whether the bag is available with left or right-hand zippers—some people prefer to zip their bags on one side or the other. A stuff sack is a standard accessory with any good bag, and some bag makers include storage sacks for those times when the bag is not in use.

OTHER EQUIPMENT

In addition to the primary items, a lot of little items need to go into your pack, even on a day hike. Although you must decide what specific gear

Hiker on the PCT takes in the view of Deep Lake and Mount Daniel.

you need and want on your outing, the folks at Washington Trails Association and I have put together checklists for day hikers and backpackers. These lists are not the last word on what to pack, but rather they are general guidelines to follow when loading up your pack. The items you have in your pack may vary from what another hiker on the same trail is carrying, but there are a few things each and every one of us should have. For instance, if you venture more than a few hundred yards away from the road, you should be prepared to spend the night under the stars (or under the clouds, as may be more likely). Mountain storms can whip up in a hurry, catching you by surprise. What was an easy-to-follow trail during a calm, clear day can disappear into a confusing world of fog and rain—or even snow—in a windy tempest. Therefore, every member of your party should have a pack loaded with the Ten Essentials and a few other items that aren't necessarily essential but are good to have on hand in an emergency.

The Ten Essentials

1. Extra clothing. This means more clothing than you would wear during the worst weather of the planned outing. If you get injured or lost, you won't be moving around generating heat, so you'll need to be able to bundle up.
2. Extra food. Pack enough that you'll have leftovers after an uneventful trip. (Those leftovers will keep you fed and fueled during an emergency.)
3. Sunglasses. While necessary for most high alpine travel, they are absolutely essential when you're traveling on or near snow.
4. Knife. There are a multitude of uses; some come easily to mind (whittling kindling for a fire; first aid applications) while others won't become apparent until you find you don't have a knife handy. A multitool is an even better option because the pliers can be used to repair damaged packs, stoves, and other gear.
5. First-aid kit. Nothing elaborate is needed—especially if you are unfamiliar with some of the uses. Make sure you have adhesive bandages, gauze bandages, some pain reliever, and so forth. A Red Cross first-aid training course is recommended.
6. Firestarter. An emergency campfire provides warmth, but it also has a calming effect on most people. Without it the night is cold, dark, and intimidating. With it, the night is held at arm's length.

A candle or tube of fire-starting ribbon is essential for starting a fire with wet wood.

7. Matches. Can't start a fire without them. Pack in a waterproof container and/or buy the waterproof/windproof variety. Book matches are useless in wind or wet weather and disposable lighters are unreliable.

8. Flashlight. If caught after dark, you'll need it to follow the trail. If forced to spend the night, you'll need it to set up emergency camp, gather wood, and so forth. Carry extra batteries and bulb.

9. Map. Carry a topographic map of the area you plan to be in and know how to read it.

10. Compass. Make sure you know how to use it.

In addition to these essentials, I add two small kit bags. One is a repair kit, containing a 20-foot length of nylon cord, a small roll of duct tape, some 1-inch webbing and extra webbing buckles (to fix broken pack straps), and a small tube of super glue. The other tiny package at the bottom of my pack is my emergency survival kit, which holds a small metal mirror, an emergency mylar "blanket," a plastic whistle, and a tiny signal smoke canister—all useful for signaling to search groups, whether they are on the ground or in the air.

DAY HIKER'S CHECKLIST

The 10+ Essentials
❑ Extra clothing (layers)
❑ Extra drinking water and food—more than you'll need during the planned hike
❑ First-aid kit
❑ Knife
❑ Matches
❑ Firestarter (candle, chemical tinders)
❑ Map
❑ Compass
❑ Flashlight and extra bulb and batteries
❑ Sunglasses and sunscreen
❑ Notebook and pencil/pen

The Basics

❏ Daypack—should be just big enough to carry all your gear

Clothing

❏ Polyester or nylon shorts/pants
❏ Short-sleeve shirts
❏ Long-sleeve shirts
❏ Warm pants (fleece or microfleece)
❏ Fleece jacket or wool sweater
❏ Wicking long underwear
❏ Noncotton underwear

Outerwear

❏ Rainwear
❏ Wide-brimmed hat for sun/rain
❏ Fleece/stocking hat for warmth
❏ Gloves (fleece/wool and shell)
❏ Bandannas

Footwear

❏ Hiking boots
❏ Hiking socks (NOT cotton)—Carry one extra pair. When your feet are soaked with sweat, change into the clean pair, rinse out the dirty pair, and hang them on the back of your pack to dry. Repeat the process as often as necessary.
❏ Liner socks—see above
❏ Extra laces
❏ Gaiters
❏ Moleskin (for prevention of blisters)
❏ Second skin (for treatment of blisters)

Optional Gear

❏ Camera
❏ Binoculars
❏ Repair kit
❏ Reading material (paperback/scary stories book)
❏ Fishing equipment
❏ Field guides (nature study)
❏ Head net/mosquito net suit

BACKPACKER'S CHECKLIST

The 10+ Essentials
❑ Extra clothing (layers)
❑ Extra drinking water and food—more than you'll need during the planned hike
❑ First-aid kit
❑ Knife
❑ Matches
❑ Firestarter (candle, chemical tinders)
❑ Map
❑ Compass
❑ Flashlight and extra bulb and batteries
❑ Sunglasses and sunscreen
❑ Notebook and pencil/pen

The Basics
❑ Backpack—internal or external (Big enough to carry all your gear with a little room left over for emergency items.)
❑ Pack raincover
❑ Tent with rainfly (don't forget stakes)
❑ Sleeping bag
❑ Sleeping pad
❑ Stove
❑ Fuel
❑ Cook set (with pot lifter)
❑ Drinking cup (insulated preferably)
❑ Utensils (for eating and cooking)
❑ Water filter or iodine tablets
❑ Water bottles
❑ Nylon cord or rope (50–100 feet)
❑ Assorted meals and snack food

Personal Hygiene
❑ Toilet paper (or small tissue package)
❑ Trowel (for "cat" hole)
❑ Toothbrush and paste
❑ Personal medication/allergy medication
❑ Small pack towel

❏ Biodegradable soap and/or "handiwipes"
❏ Insect repellent
❏ Contact solution/cleaner

Clothing
(NO COTTON ALLOWED!)
❏ Polyester or nylon shorts/pants
❏ Short-sleeve shirts
❏ Warm pants (polarfleece or wool)
❏ Fleece jacket or wool sweater
❏ Wicking long underwear
❏ Noncotton underwear (briefs, boxers, sport bra)
❏ Bandannas

Outerwear
❏ Rainwear (top and bottom)
❏ Wide-brimmed hat for sun/rain
❏ Fleece/stocking hat for warmth
❏ Gloves (fleece/wool and shell)
❏ Gaiters

Footwear
❏ Hiking boots
❏ Hiking socks (NOT cotton)—Carry one extra pair. Rinse out as
   needed to keep one pair clean.
❏ Liner socks—see above
❏ Extra laces
❏ Moleskin (for prevention of blisters)
❏ Second skin (for blister treatment)

Optional Gear
❏ Camera
❏ Binoculars
❏ Watch/alarm clock
❏ Altimeter
❏ Weather radio
❏ Repair kit
❏ Reading material
❏ Playing cards

❏ Lantern (candle or small pack lantern)
❏ Fishing equipment
❏ Field guides (nature study)
❏ Head net/mosquito net suit
❏ Tent ground sheet

FIRST-AID KIT CHECKLIST

Basic Tools
❏ Comprehensive first-aid manual
❏ Emergency blanket
❏ Magnifying glass
❏ Small mirror
❏ Tweezers
❏ Needle and thread
❏ Safety pins
❏ Scissors
❏ Small knife
❏ Razor blade
❏ Matches/lighter
❏ Thermometer
❏ Adhesive tape
❏ Duct tape

Bandages
❏ Adhesive bandages
❏ Butterfly bandages
❏ Large compress bandage
❏ Wire splint
❏ Elastic-wrap bandage (i.e., Ace bandage)
❏ Gauze pads
❏ Gauze wrap
❏ Latex safety gloves
❏ Medical tape

Medication/Treatments to Consider
❏ Antacid tablets
❏ Antibacterial ointment
❏ Antihistamine

❑ Antiseptic wipes
❑ Aspirin or pain reliever
❑ Biodegradable soap
❑ Burn ointment
❑ Calamine lotion
❑ Cough drops
❑ Eye drops
❑ Foot powder
❑ Insect repellent
❑ Iodine
❑ Lip balm
❑ Moleskin/Second skin
❑ Prescription medicines
❑ Salt tablets
❑ Snake-bite kit
❑ Sunscreen
❑ Towelettes
❑ Vitamins

GENERAL TRAIL ETIQUETTE

If you enjoy backcountry trails, you should recognize that you have a responsibility to those trails and to other trail users. We each must work to preserve the tranquillity of the wildlands, not only by being sensitive to the environment but to other trail users as well.

The PCT is open to hikers, dogs, and horse riders, but many of the side access trails are also open to mountain bikes and, occasionally, motorcycles. When you encounter other trail users, whether they are hikers, climbers, trail runners, bicyclists, or horse riders, the only hard-and-fast rule is that common sense and simple courtesy must be observed. It's hard to overstate just how vital these two qualities—common sense and courtesy—are to maintaining an enjoyable, safe, and friendly situation on our trails when different types of trail users meet.

Along with this "Golden Rule of Trail Etiquette," there are other ways in which you can make your trip, and that of the others on the trail, most enjoyable.

◆ When hikers meet other hikers, the group heading uphill has the right-of-way. There are two general reasons for this. First, on steep ascents, you tend to watch the trail before you and you

Horseback rider cresting a saddle in the ridge above Shoe Lake. The basic rule of trail etiquette is showing courtesy to other trail users.

don't notice the approach of descending hikers until you are face-to-face. Second, it is easier for descending hikers to break their stride and step off the trail than it is for those who have fallen into a good, climbing plod. If, however, you are hiking uphill and you are in need of a rest, you may step off the trail and yield the right-of-way to downhill hikers, but this is your decision as the uphill climber.

◆ When hikers meet other user groups, the hikers should move off the trail. This is because as a hiker, you are generally the most mobile and flexible user. It is easier for you to step off the trail than it is for bicyclists to lift their bikes off the trail or for horse riders to get their animals off the trail.

◆ When hikers meet horseback riders, the hikers should step off the downhill side of the trail unless the terrain makes this difficult or dangerous. If this is the case, move to the uphill side of the trail, but crouch down a bit so you do not tower over the horses' heads. Also, do not stand behind trees or brush if you can avoid it. This could make you invisible to the animals until they get close, and then your sudden appearance could startle them. Instead, stay in clear view, and talk in a normal voice to the riders. This calms the horses.

◆ Stay on trails and practice minimum impact. Don't cut switchbacks, take shortcuts, or make new trails. If your destination is off-trail, leave the trail in as direct a manner as possible. That is, move away from the trail in a line perpendicular to the trail. Once you are well clear of the trail, adjust your route to your destination.

◆ Obey the rules specific to the trail you are visiting. Many trails are closed to certain types of use, including hiking with dogs or riding horses.

◆ If you take your dog on the trails, you should have it on a leash—or under very strict voice-command—at all times.

◆ Avoid disturbing wildlife, especially in winter and in calving areas. Observe from a distance—even if you cannot get the picture you want from a distance, resist the urge to move closer to wildlife. This not only keeps you safer, but it prevents the animal from having to exert itself unnecessarily in order to flee from you.

◆ Leave all natural things and features as you found them for others to enjoy.

◆ Never roll rocks off trails or cliffs—you never know who or what is below you.

These are just a few things you can do to maintain a safe and harmonious trail environment. Remember to avoid problems by always practicing the Golden Rule of Trail Etiquette: common sense and courtesy are the order of the day.

HOW TO USE THIS BOOK

No guidebook can provide all the details of a trail, nor stay current with constantly changing conditions of trails, stream crossings, and access roads. So before you set out on any hike, call the land manager for the latest information on trail conditions—you'll find the phone numbers in Appendix A. Current trail conditions for the PCT are available toll-free at (888) PCTRAIL [728-7245] and are posted on the PCTA website, *www.pcta.org*, from April 1 through October 31.

You'll also find references to the Green Trails map quadrants covering the described hike. Green Trails, Inc., uses the standard 7.5-minute United States Geological Service (USGS) topographical maps as their starting point, but where USGS maps may not have been updated since sometime in the 1950s, the Green Trails cartographers have researchers in the field every year, checking trail conditions and changes. Many hikers still use the USGS maps for their hiking, and they work when you are looking at the mountains and contours since the natural features don't change rapidly. But the man-made features do change, and I think Green Trails does the best job of all the mapmakers in staying abreast of those changes.

When referring to the hiking time, please bear in mind that this is an estimation based on my experience on the trail and the speed at which I expect the average hiker to travel. You may find my estimates are too high or too low. I encourage you to use my estimated time as a tool to help you plan your hike and not as a gauge with which to measure your success or failure.

The seasonal listing is another subjective tool meant to be a guide and not an absolute. Some years (such as 1999) the heavy winter snowpack doesn't melt off the high country until early September. In other years, the highest trails may be snow-free by the Fourth of July. Again, use this information as a tool to help you plan your trips, and then call the land manager to get the latest information on trail conditions.

ENJOY THE TRAILS

Above all else, I hope you safely enjoy the trails in this book. If you achieve even a fraction of the pleasure I have found on the Pacific Crest Trail and its side trails, then you will be blessed with wonderful outings. These trails exist for our enjoyment, and for the enjoyment of future generations. We can use them and protect them at the same time if we are careful with our actions and forthright with our demands on Congress to continue and further the protection of our country's wildlands.

Throughout the twentieth century, wilderness lovers helped secure protection for the lands we love today. As we enter the twenty-first century, we must see to it that protection continues and that the last bits of wildlands are also preserved for the enjoyment of future generations.

Please, if you value these trails, get involved. Something as simple as writing a letter to your representative in Congress can make a big difference.

PANTHER CREEK EXPERIMENTAL FOREST

Distance: 7.2 miles round trip	
Hiking time: 5 hours (day hike)	
High point: 4,000 feet	
Elevation gain: 1,200 feet	
Season: April through June or September through November	
Map: Green Trails Wind River, No. 397	
Land manager: Wind River Ranger District	

Images of high ridges and towering peaks often come to mind when the words *Pacific Crest Trail* are uttered; however, this section of trail provides a contrasting, but no less beautiful, image to consider. The Panther Creek Experimental Forest is a protected area of old, open pine and fir forest. The PCT rolls along the south and east sides of the forest preserve. The woods are teeming with wildlife and remarkably lacking in human visitors, making this a wonderful hike on which to find solitude and an opportunity to see a variety of birds and animals. During a visit in late September, I counted no less than a dozen species of birds, including downy woodpeckers, ravens, siskins, a mountain bluebird, an oriole, and

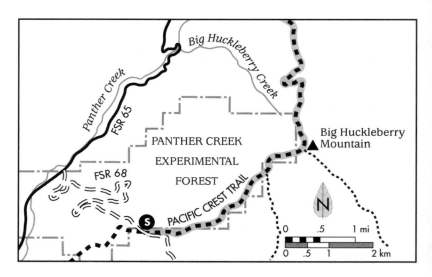

a Cooper's hawk. Among the animals I saw were deer, rabbits, and squirrels. I also noted the tracks of a big coyote, and on my return, I found the tracks of a cougar overlaying my earlier footprints. I didn't see these critters, but I was certainly seen by them.

Dry, open forest along the Panther Creek section of the PCT

To get there, from Carson drive north on the Wind River Road 5.6 miles and turn right (east) onto Panther Creek Road (FSR 65). Continue on Panther Creek Road about 4 miles to a junction with FSR 68. Make a sharp right turn and begin a steep ascent of Road 68. In 2 miles, at the crown of the hill, pull off into the PCT trailhead parking area on the right.

The PCT comes in from the south along an old jeep track, crosses FSR 68, and enters the Panther Creek Experimental Forest as a narrow, little-used path. The trail climbs through a pair of switchbacks in the first .5 mile, then rolls into a long climbing traverse along a wooded ridge. In 2.6 miles, a junction with a small side trail (Cedar Creek Trail) is reached. Stay left on the PCT for another mile or so to reach the flanks of Big Huckleberry Mountain and the junction with Dog Mountain Trail. There is no path to the top of Big Huckleberry Mountain, and little reason to attempt to reach the forested top. Rather, stick to the huge sun-dappled clearings in the forest along the trail to enjoy the bright sunshine, colorful flowers, and—in later summer and early autumn—the abundant huckleberries.

The forest is somewhat sparse, with huge openings in the canopy allowing great beams of sunlight to illuminate the forest floor. Beargrass blooms along the trail in early spring, while Oregon grape and huckleberries color the hillside in autumn. The route is dry, so pack plenty of water. Return the way you came.

BIG LAVA BED TO BIG HUCKLEBERRY MOUNTAIN

Distance: 13 miles round trip	
Hiking time: 7 hours (day hike)	
High point: 4,000 feet	
Elevation gain: 600 feet	
Season: April through June or September through November	
Map: Green Trails Wind River, No. 397	
Land manager: Mount Adams Ranger District	

Start big and end big. This route begins by skirting Big Lava Bed and ends at Big Huckleberry Mountain. Neither landmark is what might be expected along the Pacific "Crest" Trail, but there they are—more solid evidence that the PCT is indeed a wonderfully diverse route.

Big Lava Bed is the home of an old lava flow. Magma oozed out of

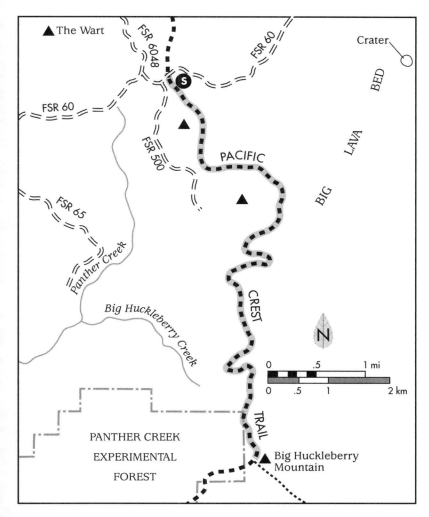

fissures and cracks in the heart of the Lava Bed, as well as along the lower flanks of Mount Adams, in the southern Indian Heaven Wilderness Area, and of course, around Mount St. Helens. The flows began some 9,000 years ago, and as Mount St. Helens showed in 1980, volcanic activity in the area is still occurring. Big Lava Bed is a volcanic formation, but it's not the classic conical volcano. Rather, the bed is a 20-square-mile flow of basalt that came up out of a source vent found in the north-central part of the bed, just south of Goose Lake.

To get there, from Carson drive north on Wind River Road 5.6 miles and turn right (east) onto Panther Creek Road (FSR 65). Continue on Panther Creek Road 11.3 miles to a junction with FSR 60. Turn right (east) onto FSR 60 and drive 2.4 miles to the horse camp on the right. The PCT crosses FSR 60 here. Find the start of the trail to the south just behind the outhouses on the south side of the horse camp.

Spindly pines cover much of the Lava Bed, giving it the appearance of a gentle, young forest from a distance. Get near the lava, though, and the truth comes out. There is nothing gentle about this landscape.

The PCT skirts the west side of the basalt field and almost immediately after starting the hike, the harsh nature of the lava bed is starkly evident. Step off-trail and the landscape is nearly impassable. The lava is abrasive, brittle, and very unstable. Try to scramble to the top of one of the short lava knobs scattered around the area and you'll find your leather boots not just scuffed but slashed and cut to ribbons. Better to enjoy the rugged beauty of the lava flow from the relative safety of the trail.

The trail leaves the horse camp and within the first .25 mile meets the lava flows. The trail then rolls with the flow, so to speak, skirting the rough lava on its western flank. To the west of the trail is an open pine forest scarred with clearcuts, but the buffer of trees along the trail blocks most of that logging damage from view. Besides, the lava beds will keep your eyes turned away from the other side of the trail.

The terrain in the Big Lava Bed is a jumble of rock. Huge blocks of lava, towering up like black cotton-candy tufts, dot the landscape. Many of these are pahoehoe formations—wrinkled masses of rock

Looking north over Big Lava Bed toward Red Mountain

formed by fast-moving lava. Pahoehoe is easy to identify by its solid mass of ropy folds and wrinkles. Or just look for the rocks that remind you of shar pei dogs. Between the great tufts of lava are fissures, crevices, pressure ridges, and fields of sharp, jagged black basalt.

The trail follows alongside this world of volcanic turmoil for nearly 3 miles before edging away from the lava into a calmer world of pine forests. The trail rolls gently through the forest for another 3.5 miles to the flank of Big Huckleberry Mountain. Turn around where the trail leaves the lava for a short outing, or proceed to Big Huckleberry Mountain, for a full day of hiking. The mountain is aptly named—in late summer the surrounding area is flush with marble-sized purple fruit.

Return to the trailhead by the same route.

3 GIFFORD PEAK

Distance: 11.6 miles round trip	
Hiking time: 6 hours (day hike)	
High point: 5,000 feet	
Elevation gain: 700 feet	
Season: Late summer	
Map: Green Trails Wind River, No. 397	
Land manager: Mount Adams Ranger District	

The Indian Heaven Wilderness Area is tiny compared to some of the wilderness preserves in Washington, but don't let its size fool you. This area is a rare gem with its multitude of sparkling lakes, acres of flower-filled meadows, fields of rich berries, and herds of deer and elk. There are many ways to enter the tiny wilderness, but from the south, the most scenic access is from the top of Red Mountain, a cinder-cone volcano.

The trail starts high, and the elevation doesn't change much along the route's length as the trail follows ridges north. The route leads past a historic gathering place of Northwest tribes—the Indian Racetrack—and traverses a long ridge before ending in the shadow of another volcano, Gifford Peak.

To get there, from Carson drive north on Wind River Road 5.6 miles and then turn right (east) onto Panther Creek Road (FSR 65). Continue

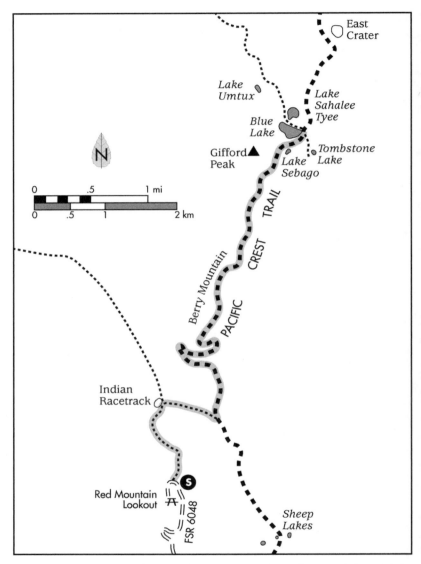

on Panther Creek Road 11.3 miles to a junction with FSR 60. Turn right (east) onto FSR 60 and drive 1.6 miles to the junction with FSR 6048. Turn left, and drive 4 miles to the end of the road. Note: This is a one-lane dirt road. High-clearance vehicles are required, and when conditions are wet, four-wheel drive is recommended.

Deep Lake near Gifford Peak in the Indian Heaven Wilderness

A still-active lookout tower sits atop Red Mountain, and it is worth a few minutes' delay to trek up to the lookout cabin before beginning the hike. Astounding views of the volcanic landscape of the South Cascades are found from the cabin. Mount St. Helens, Mount Hood, and Mount Adams line the horizons. The giant scab of the Big Lava Bed sprawls at your feet to the southeast and a host of little cinder cones dot the countryside all around—most notably, The Wart to the south and the crater cone in the center of the lava bed to the east.

The trailhead is about a hundred yards below the summit, at the last hairpin turn in the road. The trail heads due north for 1 mile to reach a junction with the Indian Racetrack Trail at the racetrack itself. This first leg of the hike is a gradual descent along a ridgeline, mostly in scrub pine and open meadow. As the trail nears the racetrack, the forest closes in and the trail levels out. The racetrack itself is a meadow area where native horsemen from various tribes competed. The area was a popular gathering ground for a number of native peoples because of its rich abundance of fish, berries, big game, and a variety of roots and tubers. Every year tribes would gather to harvest the food to stock up for winter, as well as to trade goods and news with other tribes, and of course, to race. The racetrack is a deep impression in the turf that is slowly fading under the encroaching plant life of the rich meadow.

At the junction with the Racetrack Trail, go right (east) on Trail No. 171A and in .5 mile, reach the PCT. Turn north (left) on the PCT and begin a gradual climb to the crest of Berry Mountain—a long, jagged ridge. Berry Mountain, a volcanic formation, is what remains of vast lava vents that spewed molten basalt onto the land surface. The trail rides the crest of this mountain north. About 4 miles from the trailhead, the trail crosses the true summit of Berry Mountain—5,000 feet—and starts a gentle descent to Blue Lake at the foot of Gifford Peak. Fine camping is available at the lake, and good huckleberry thickets are all along the trail.

In addition to the wonderful berries found in late spring, this section of the PCT offers a great lesson in the volcanic nature of the South Cascades. Not only does this leg of the PCT cross volcanic mountains at its beginning, middle, and end, but it also offers wonderful views of a host of nearby volcanoes—from the towering snow-clad peak of Mount Adams to the tiny tree-clad peak of The Wart.

Return the way you came.

4 BIRD MOUNTAIN LOOP

Distance: 6.7-mile loop (or extended loop of 10.2 miles)
Hiking time: 5 hours (day hike or backpack)
High point: 5,200 feet
Elevation gain: 1,200 feet
Season: Late summer
Map: Green Trails Lone Butte, No. 365
Land manager: Mount Adams Ranger District

Indian Heaven Wilderness Area is a wonderland of sparkling lakes, jagged peaks, open forests, and most notably, sprawling meadows filled with flowers and an array of wildlife. A pair of loop trails around Bird Mountain—

View east to Mount Adams from the flank of Bird Mountain

the highest peak in the wilderness—allows you to experience the best of each of those offerings. The short loop stays close to the flank of Bird Mountain, while the longer loop wanders farther south into bigger meadowlands before turning back to skirt around the mountain.

To get there, from Bingen on SR 14 take SR 141 north to Trout Lake. From there continue on SR 141 west for about 8 miles to Peterson Prairie Campground and a junction with FSR 24. Turn right onto FSR 24 and

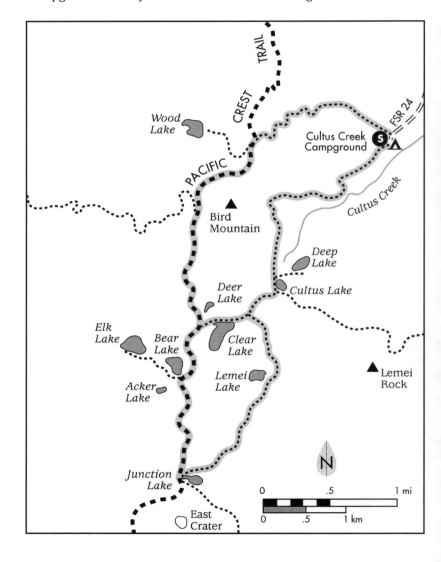

drive 5.5 miles to the Cultus Creek Campground on the left. The starting trailhead is found near the back of the campground loop.

This loop is best done clockwise, so begin on the Cultus Creek Trail (No. 33) and start a long, steep climb to the east flank of Bird Mountain. The first 1.5 miles gain nearly 1,200 feet in elevation as the trail ruthlessly ascends the Cultus Creek Valley. About 1 mile into the hike, the trail breaks out on a small ridge. Look east from this rocky point and Mount Adams dominates the horizon. Below the viewpoint, the slope drops steeply away and rolls into a long blanket of green between the base of Bird Mountain and the flank of Mount Adams. Face north on clear days and Mount Rainier can be seen. Between the two great volcanoes sprawl the craggy summits of the Goat Rocks Wilderness Area.

From here the trail turns sharply south as it draws near the cliff faces of Bird Mountain. Pine forests enclose the trail, with occasional meadow breaks and views of the towering cliffs, until the trail passes the crystal clear waters of Cultus Lake at 2.5 miles. This is a fine lake in which to swim or to just enjoy from the shore during a leisurely lunch. Beyond the lake, Lemei Rock scrapes the sky. This 5,925-foot rock is the remnant plug from the core of a long-gone volcano.

A side trail leaves to the left just a few hundred feet beyond the lake. This path leads to Lemei Rock and beyond. Stay right on the main trail, and in another .25 mile, reach a second trail junction. This is Lemei Lake Trail, No. 179, the split between the long and short loops.

If you are planning to do the longer loop turn left and continue south on this trail. It leads past Lemei Lake—a shallow, somewhat dirty lake— and angles through a series of meadows and wooded sections before reaching Junction Lake at 5.9 miles from the trailhead. Junction Lake, so-named because two side trails merge into the PCT at the lakeshore, is a muddy, frog-filled pond at the base of East Crater. This cinder-cone volcano is heavily wooded with spindly pines, and though no trail leads to the top, it is possible to bushwhack to its summit for a view of the crater for which the formation is named.

In autumn, when the mosquito population and the water levels are both down, fine camping can be found in the meadows around the lake. In midsummer, though, this is a boggy, bug-filled basin. Better to hustle through to clearer lakes and breezier (i.e., bug-free) locations.

Turn north (right) at Junction Lake onto the PCT. The trail heads due north along the edge of a wooded ridge. For a bit of variety, hop off the trail and explore the huge meadows seen to the west, just below the trail.

Deer, elk, and a variety of small mammals thrive in these fields of grass and wildflowers. The meadows are crisscrossed with horse and game trails, so knowing the location of the main trail is imperative. A map and compass are essential tools for exploring off-trail.

One mile north of Junction Lake, the PCT passes Bear Lake and a side trail to Elk Lake on the left. The forest thickens and closes in around the trail for the next .5 mile as the route climbs toward Bird Mountain and a junction with Trail No. 33.

If you are hiking the short loop, you'll join the PCT here. From the junction where the long hike splits off to this junction, Trail No. 33 rolls less than .5 mile through woods and scree slopes at the base of Bird Mountain to reach the PCT. (In comparison, the long loop covered 3.5 miles.)

The PCT heads north from this junction, angling east toward the rocky upper slopes of Bird Mountain. Just beyond Wood Lake Trail Junction, leave the PCT by bearing right onto Trail No. 108, which leads back to Cultus Creek Campground in another 1.5 miles. Before heading for the trailhead though, stop at the ridge crest just after leaving the PCT and enjoy the views. Or, for markedly better views, climb south along the ridge until the whole of the South Cascades is spread out in all its splendor. Mount St. Helens, Mount Rainier, the Goat Rocks Peaks, and Mount Adams can be seen on clear days from this vantage point, less than .25 mile off the trail. Don't bother risking the scramble to the summit of Bird Mountain because the views are no better from that higher, more dangerous perch.

The trail back to the trailhead is a steep descent through trees, ending at the Cultus Creek Campground entrance.

5 INDIAN HEAVEN TRAVERSE

Distance: 17.1 miles one way	
Hiking time: Allow 2 days	
High point: 5,000 feet	
Elevation gain: 1,600 feet	
Season: Late summer	
Maps: Green Trails Wind River, No. 397, and Lone Butte, No. 365	
Land manager: Mount Adams Ranger District	

The PCT pierces through the heart of the Indian Heaven Wilderness Area, a largely undiscovered jewel in the South Cascades. The wilderness area

Indian Heaven Wilderness is a land of lakes, including Clear Lake, seen here.

is just 20,650 acres, with huge sprawling meadows (watch for elk and big mule deer), lush huckleberry fields, and a variety of volcanic elements to view and explore.

To get there, from Carson drive north on Wind River Road 5.6 miles and turn right (east) onto Panther Creek Road (FSR 65). Continue on Panther Creek Road 11.3 miles to a junction with FSR 60. Turn right (east) onto FSR 60 and drive 2.4 miles to the horse camp on the right. The PCT crosses FSR 60 here. Find the start of the trail on the north side of the road, opposite the entrance to the horse camp. To reach the northern terminus, from White Salmon on SR 14 take SR 141 north to Trout Lake. Continue on SR 141 heading west for about 8 miles to Peterson Prairie Campground and a junction with FSR 24. Turn right onto FSR 24 and drive about 10 miles north to the point where the PCT crosses the road near Surprise Lake Campground.

Hiking south to north, the trail leaves the Big Lava Bed and crosses a series of rolling, forest-covered hills (with the occasional clearcut to mar the view) in the first couple of miles before entering the wilderness near Sheep Lakes. At 3.5 miles, the PCT meets the Indian Racetrack Trail on the left. The trail climbs gently, gaining a mere 900 feet in those 3.5 miles. The next stretch climbs a little more aggressively as the trail leads up the long meadow-lined ridge of Berry Mountain, crossing the mountain summit at 5,000 feet. A drop through more pine forest leads to Blue Lake at the foot of Gifford Peak 8 miles from the trailhead.

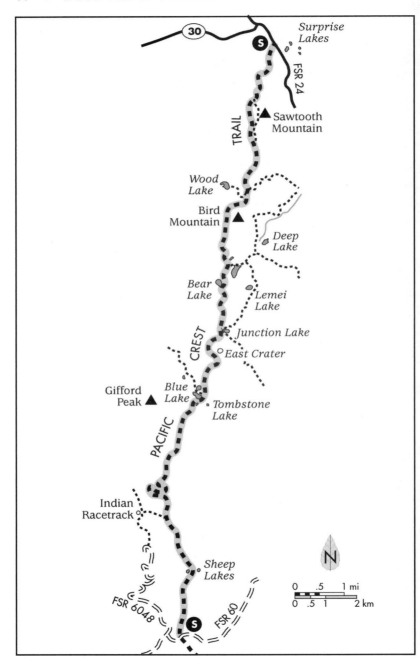

From Blue Lake, stick to the right fork (the left fork leads to Eunice, Heather, and Thomas Lakes) and follow the PCT along the west slope of East Crater to reach Junction Lake at 10.2 miles. North of Junction Lake, the PCT skirts the eastern edge of a series of sprawling meadows—drop off the trail and explore these for possible views of browsing deer and elk, or maybe soaring raptors overhead. The trail continues north past Bear Lake, entering thick pine forests before reaching the foot of Bird Mountain.

Scree slopes, alpine meadows, and open forest line the trail as it traverses the western flank of Bird Mountain. At the north end of the mountain, near the junction with Wood Lake Trail, find good views of the grand peaks of the South Cascades. The panorama includes Mount Adams, the Goat Rocks, Mount Rainier, and Mount St. Helens on clear days.

North of Wood Lake Trail junction, the PCT descends gradually through trees for a mile before splitting. Parallel trails lead around the flank of Sawtooth Mountain. The eastern trail, covering 2 miles, climbs steeply toward the 5,323-foot summit, followed by an equally steep descent. Meanwhile, the western trail maintains a level traverse along the mountain's flank, covering only 1 mile. The two paths rejoin just inside the wilderness boundary and continue north for 1.4 miles through open forest to the north trailhead at FSR 24 near Surprise Lakes Campground.

6 THE BUMPER

Distance: 10 miles round trip	
Hiking time: 6 hours (day hike or backpack)	
High point: 6,100 feet	
Elevation gain: 1,900 feet	
Season: Late summer or early fall	
Map: Green Trails Mount Adams, No. 367S	
Land manager: Mount Adams Ranger District	

Mount Adams towers over the South Cascades. The big stratovolcano rises out of a sprawling jumble of lava beds that make cross-country trails difficult along the flanks of the big mountain. But those same lava flows add a wonderful scenic element to trail hiking. Snow-capped Mount Adams fills the horizon, but at its feet is a world of jagged black

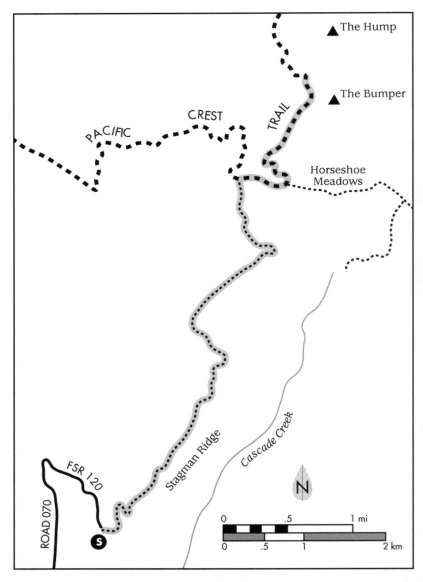

rock that slashes at the boots and hands of any adventurer careless enough to scramble off-trail.

This route offers a wonderful introduction to the diversity of the PCT in a relatively short hike. Do it as a long hike, a simple overnight backpacking trip, or set up a basecamp at one of the fine campsites along the way and enjoy a few days exploring the flank of the big volcano.

The trail begins high on a ridge covered with old-growth pine and climbs steeply to the rock and ice of the alpine world. Along the way, the trail offers views of rushing rivers and hanging glaciers, cool forests and sun-filled flower meadows, fields of berries and herds of deer and elk.

To get there, from White Salmon on SR 14 head north to Trout Lake on SR 141. Drive north on FSR 23 for about 8.5 miles and turn right (east) onto FSR 8031. In about .25 mile, bear left onto Spur Road 070 and drive about 3 miles to another road junction. Turn right onto FSR 120 and follow it to the trailhead at the road end, less than 1 mile farther on.

The trail leaves the clearcuts near the road end and climbs to the wilderness boundary in the first .25 mile. From there, the path rides the sharp spine of Stagman Ridge. Ancient pine forests shade the ridge crest, but the sheer drop to the south is apparent, even in the cool shadows of the forest. The ridge slopes gently away to the north, but its southern face drops almost vertically more than 1,000 feet to the bottom of the Cascade Creek Valley.

This precipitous ridge walk continues for just about 1.5 miles before the trail angles north away from the cliff top and heads into deeper forest. At 2 miles, the way crosses a thundering (in early summer) creek at 5,100 feet and begins a gentle 2-mile climb to Horseshoe Meadows at 5,800 feet.

The Stagman Ridge Trail joins the PCT about .5 mile west of Horseshoe Meadows amid splendid views of Mount Adams. From the broad, flower-filled meadows, White Salmon Glacier, Avalanche Glacier, and the mountain's true summit are all seen from the clearings here. Leaving

Lava on the flanks of Mount Adams

Horseshoe Meadows (5,900 feet), the PCT climbs gradually for another 2 miles through alpine meadow and open stands of timber. At 6,100 feet, the trail is at timberline on the western edge of The Bumper—a knob of basalt at the edge of the trees.

It's possible to scramble to the top of the 6,490-foot rock, but be warned that the lava rock is sharp and brittle. Hands, clothing, and even boot leather are all at risk. The jagged rock will slice and dice faster than any machine sold on a late-night infomercial.

View The Bumper and its adjacent lava fields at the foot of Mount Adams before heading back down the trail the way you came. If you are backpacking, you will find fine campsites throughout the Horseshoe Meadows area. Water can be found in the small streams and seeps scattered around the meadows.

7 LOOKING GLASS LAKE

Distance: 16 miles round trip	
Hiking time: 2 or more days	
High point: 6,000 feet	
Elevation gain: 2,400 feet	
Season: Late summer	
Map: Green Trails Mount Adams, No. 367S	
Land manager: Mount Adams Ranger District	

Pine forests give way to basalt lava beds as you climb east along the PCT to the timberline on graceful Mount Adams. This wonderfully formed mountain is one of the youngest of the big volcanoes, and as such, hasn't yet lost its smooth cone shape to the forces of erosion. The only scenario that could make the mountain more attractive is to see it reflected in the transparent waters of a wilderness lake. Looking Glass can't truthfully be called a lake—it's far too small for that—but when the winds are calm and the air is clear, the tiny tarn does reflect the face of Adams as well as any looking glass.

This hike offers a lot more than a mere reflection, however. The trail climbs through young pine forests, crosses broad meadows, and skirts jagged lava beds along its way to the lake. Making Looking Glass a basecamp, you can explore north along the PCT to The Hump or Crystal

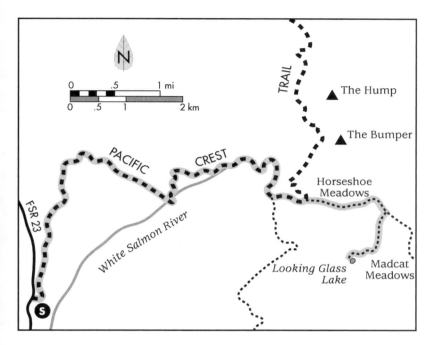

Lake just off the trail at the edge of the lava fields, or you can hike south along the Round the Mountain Trail to see the wildflower fields of Madcat Meadows.

To get there, from White Salmon on SR 14 head north on SR 141 to Trout Lake. Drive north on FSR 23 for about 13.5 miles to the PCT trailhead and turn right onto a small dirt road marked PCT North Trailhead. Follow this a few hundred yards to a trailhead parking lot.

Follow the trail east into the pine forest above the road. The trail rolls gently uphill for .5 mile or so before steepening for a long climb north along the ridge above the White Salmon River. At 2 miles, the trail crosses into the Mount Adams Wilderness Area and hooks back to the east. Views in the first couple of miles are limited to the surrounding forest, with its dark pines and firs. Great horned owls, woodpeckers, and Clark's nutcrackers, among a host of other bird species, are found in these woods, as are blacktail deer. The deer in this part of the Cascades are something of a cross between the small "coastal" blacktail found throughout the wet forests of western Washington and the bigger Rocky Mountain variety of blacktail better known as mule deer.

Once in the wilderness, the trail levels out briefly and angles south-east about 1 mile to cross the headwaters of the White Salmon River before starting a grueling climb up the steep slope of Mount Adams. Few switchbacks exist as the trail pushes up, up, up. At 5.6 miles, the trail forks. Stay left, and enter a world of sloping alpine meadows. In just under .5 mile from the junction, the trail is in the heart of Horseshoe Meadows with views of Mount Adams looming to the east. White Salmon Glacier, Avalanche Glacier, and the mountain's true summit can all be seen from the clearings. The PCT turns north here while the Round the Mountain Trail heads south. As the name implies, the Round the Mountain Trail loops completely around Mount Adams, although the eastern half of the trail is poorly marked and difficult to follow through the section within the Yakama Indian Reservation.

Looking Glass Trail near the PCT skirts the flank of Mount Adams.

Leave the PCT at the meadows, and follow the Round the Mountain Trail (Trail No. 9) southeast about 1 mile to a small trail junction on the right. One mile south on this spur leads to the trail's end at the little pond that is Looking Glass Lake. Camp here or back at the meadows. If you plan on staying multiple days, you can use your camp as a base of operations for day hikes.

If you are a basecamper, start to explore the area by heading south along the Round the Mountain Trail. The best views are found to the south. From the junction of the Looking Glass Lake Trail and the Round the Mountain Trail, head south about 1.5 miles to where the trail crosses a field of black basaltic lava. Mount Adams towers above, with Avalanche Glacier directly above the lava bed. To the left of the glacier is a huge scar on the rocks—the scene of a massive 1997 landslide that brought hundreds of tons of rock and ice down with it.

Return to the trailhead the way you came.

8 SHEEP LAKE / BURNT ROCK

Distance: 13 miles round trip	
Hiking time: 7 hours, (day hike or backpack)	
High point: 6,100 feet	
Elevation gain: 1,400 feet	
Season: Late summer	
Map: Green Trails Mount Adams, No. 367S	
Land manager: Mount Adams Ranger District	

Burnt Rock is an appropriate name for the black mound of basalt piled up near Sheep Lake. The rock is one of the many upthrusts of volcanic rock in this area of massive lava beds, and Sheep Lake is a cool pool of sparkling water nestled in the folds of lava near the base of Burnt Rock. The route to the two landforms slices in a nearly straight line from the trailhead to the PCT at timberline, and then follows the PCT south to the lakeshore. Along the way, the trail passes a few small barren lava beds, some deep old-growth pine and cedar forests, and fields of huckleberries big enough to satisfy the hunger of a battalion of bears and an army of hikers. The berries of Mount Adams are legendary for their size, number, and sweet sun-enriched flavor. Berry bushes line this route from start to finish, sometimes in small clumps in the open forest, sometimes

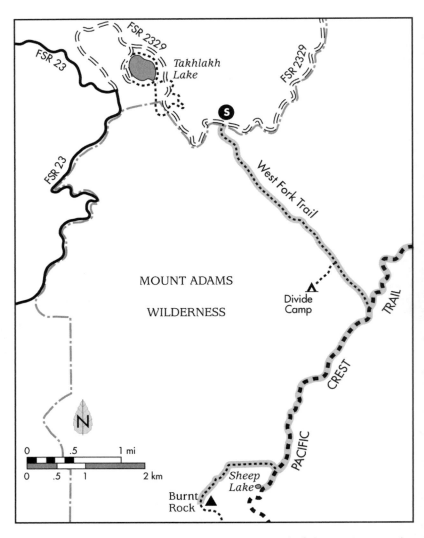

in vast berry patches in the clearings. It's a wonderful experience to be able to hike all day, nibbling on juicy fruit as you walk, with spectacular views of the snow-capped mountain before you.

To get there, from Randle on US 12, drive south on FSR 23/25. One mile from Randle, bear left onto FSR 23 and drive 32 miles to a junction with FSR 2329 (signed Takhlakh Lake Campground) and turn left onto FSR 2329. Continue 3.5 miles to the West Fork Trailhead on the right, at elevation 4,700 feet.

The trail begins at the wilderness boundary and climbs modestly through old-growth pine and spruce forests for nearly 2 miles. In the first mile, a small lava bed can be seen through the trees to the right of the trail—it looks like a black gravel pile from a distance, but if you scramble over for a closer look, you'll find it is more like a black boulder pile. Huge blocks of jagged basalt rock are piled haphazardly around the field, left by a flow of molten lava coming from a vent in the side of the mountain. The route occasionally drops close to the crashing waters of the West Fork of Adams Creek, but it generally stays on the slope above.

At 1.8 miles, you'll pass a small side trail, which leads south about .5 mile to a pretty campsite at the edge of a meadow known as Divide Camp. One mile past this spur trail, the West Fork Trail ends in a broad meadow at a junction with the PCT. High above the PCT to the east is the white monolith of Adams Glacier, headwaters of Adams Creek. Turning south (right) on the PCT, you'll hike along the upper edge of the heather-filled meadow, staying near the line where lush meadow gives way to a world of rock and ice.

The trail stays near the 6,100-foot level for nearly 1.5 miles before crossing a .5-mile-wide lava bed. Stay on the trail as it cuts through this jumble of lava because the black rocks of the bed are brittle and often razor sharp. Trying to hike cross-country in a lava bed is a sure-fire way to turn a good pair of leather boots into a shredded pair of leather boots. If you do want to explore the lava bed, bring along a sturdy pair of leather gloves—without protection, your hands could be scratched, scraped, and even deeply cut by sharp-edged rocks. Don't venture out onto the bed without a dependable compass.

A post-marking for the PCT, with the PCT logo branded into the post top

The PCT descends gradually just past the lava bed, dropping to another trail junction at 5,700 feet (6.1 miles from the trailhead). Stay left to remain on the PCT, and in another .25 mile, you'll reach the small pool of Sheep Lake. Good campsites can be found here. An alternative is to bear right at the last trail junction and hike about 1 mile through open meadows, crossing Riley Creek, to reach the west side of Burnt Rock.

Deer, elk, and mountain goats frequent the meadows between Burnt Rock and Sheep Lake. Because of the abundance of huckleberries in the well-watered meadows, bears are also frequent visitors to the area. Use proper bear-bagging techniques when camping here.

Return the way you came.

9 HIGH CAMP / KILLEN MEADOWS

Distance: 10 miles round trip

Hiking time: 6 hours (day hike or backpack)

High point: 6,900 feet

Elevation gain: 2,300 feet

Season: Late summer

Map: Green Trails Mount Adams, No. 367S

Land manager: Mount Adams Ranger District

Meadows. Lush, green meadows filled with fragrant wildflowers and juicy berries. High alpine meadows with low, hardy heathers and grasses. Subalpine meadows littered with rocks and patches of slow-melting snow. This route explores a rich cornucopia of meadow types.

But these natural pasturelands for wildlife aren't the only draws to this route. From start to finish, the trail here offers outstanding views of Mount Adams and its many personalities. The rocky cliff faces, the crevasse-torn glaciers, the flowing white snowfields, and the noble crown of the summit are all visible most of the way up the trail. As you return back down the trail, you'll face the older, more scarred cone of Mount Rainier and the gaping maw at the top of Mount St. Helens.

To get there, from Randle on US 12, drive 1 mile south on FSR 23/25. At the first main road junction, bear left onto FSR 23 and drive 32 miles to a junction with FSR 2329 (signed Takhlakh Lake Campground) and turn left onto FSR 2329. Continue 6 miles to the Killen Creek Trailhead on the right, at elevation 4,580 feet.

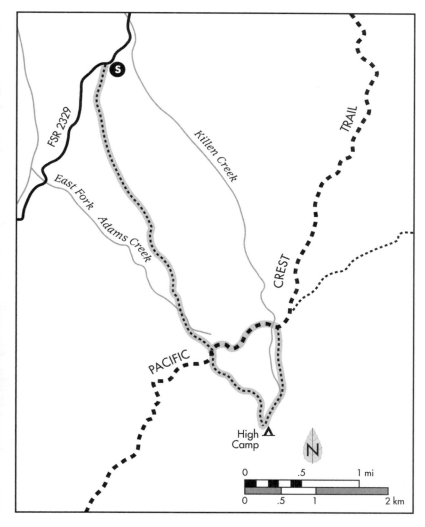

Step onto the trail and immediately enter a wonderland of color. Wildflowers grace the meadows and open forest along the trail for most of its length, and throughout much of the hiking season. Early in the season, the bulbous blooms of beargrass wave you on, while later in the summer, the trail is lit with brilliant displays of gaudy colors, thanks to the prolific wildflowers, including paintbrush, marsh marigolds, shooting stars, columbine, and lupine, to name just a few. The trail climbs gradually through forest clearings and open, sun-dappled stands of old growth for the initial 2 miles before running into a denser, cooler forest of old growth. This ancient cathedral continues for less than 1 mile before the way opens once more onto bright, sunlit meadows with glorious views of Mount Adams ahead.

At just over 2.5 miles, the trail crosses a stream in the meadow—East Fork Adams Creek—and reaches the first of the countless possibilities for camping. This is the start of the sprawling meadow country, and the broad fields around East Fork Adams Creek are quite properly known as the Adams Creek Meadows. Scramble off away from the trail to find a suitable, solitary campsite here, and then spend days exploring the rest of the area from your basecamp, or if you must, press on.

At just over 3 miles, the Killen Creek Trail dead-ends at the PCT, at 6,100-feet elevation amidst heather meadows with wide-open views of Mount Adams. A faint way-trail leads seemingly straight toward the summit from this junction. This is the route to High Camp, a rocky plateau at the edge of the life zone—the line where vegetation gives way to a world of rock and ice. High Camp, at 6,900 feet, is often crowded on hot August weekends, so it's usually best to camp lower and visit High Camp as a side trip.

The trail to High Camp covers the 800-foot gain in just 1 mile, and a second trail, about 1.3 miles long, descends to the northeast along the headwaters of Killen Creek to join the PCT near its junction with the Highline Trail at 5,900 feet.

At this junction, Killen Creek tumbles north through green meadows. A slew of ponds and small pools dot the meadows, and good campsites can be found on the higher

Huckleberries along Killen Creek Trail near the Pacific Crest Trail

knolls of Killen Meadows. To return to the trailhead, hike west along the PCT about 1.3 miles back to the Killen Creek Trail junction.

10 MOUNT ADAMS THRU HIKE

Distance: 23.8 miles one way

Hiking time: 2 to 3 days

High point: 6,100 feet

Elevation gain: 2,500 feet

Season: Late summer

Map: Green Trails Mount Adams, No. 367S

Land manager: Mount Adams Ranger District

Mount Adams, at 12,276 feet, dominates the South Cascades and provides the most dramatic scenery along the southernmost section of the PCT. The mountain first formed nearly a million years ago, about 3 miles southeast of its current location. That first cone was ground down by glaciers during the long succession of ice ages that swept the region, while the "hot spot" that gave birth to the mountain shifted northwest as plate tectonics and continental drift rearranged the landscape.

Today, the steep-sided Ridge of Wonders stands near the old core plug on the southeast side of Mount Adams. The modern mountain started forming about a half million years ago, and it is still actively building, as are a host of small cinder cones and shield volcanoes around its base. Many of these can be seen from the long stretch of the PCT that skirts the western flank of the mountain.

The trail climbs through dry, cathedral-like old-growth pine forests and traverses sprawling meadows of wildflowers. The trail knifes through jagged piles of basalt in massive, old lava beds, and it slides under massive glaciers hugging the upper slopes of the mountain.

The Mount Adams Wilderness Area encompasses all but 4 miles of this stretch of the PCT—2 miles on either end—and as a result, the route is wild and pristine. Not only are the landscape and flora remarkably beautiful and unsullied but so too is the wildlife. The region is home to some of the most impressive megafauna—the big, beautiful animals everyone loves to see—including blacktail deer, mule deer, elk, mountain goats, black bears, cougars, coyotes, and bobcats. But there is also a

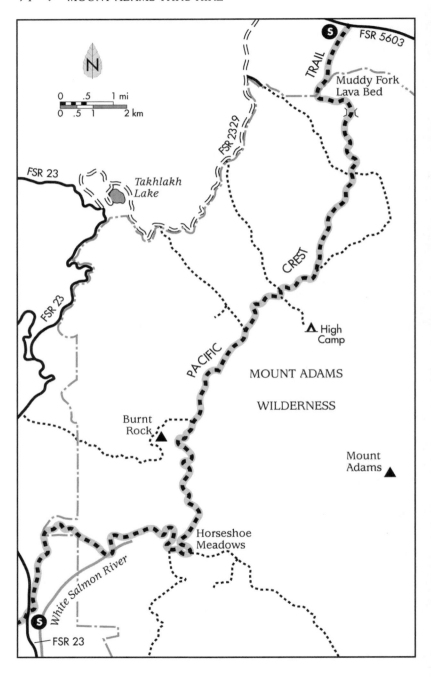

wonderful diversity of smaller mammals—marmots, pikas, weasels, martens, raccoons, porcupines, badgers—and other critters you might not expect in volcanic country, including tree frogs, western toads, alligator lizards, and rubber boa snakes.

To get to the southern trailhead, from White Salmon on SR 14 head north on SR 141 to Trout Lake. Drive north on FSR 23 for about 13.5 miles to the PCT trailhead and turn right onto a small dirt road marked PCT North Trailhead. Follow this a few hundred yards to a trailhead parking lot. To reach the north trailhead, continue north on FSR 23 another 10 miles past the southern trailhead and turn right (east) onto FSR 2329 (signed Takhlakh Lake Campground). Follow FSR 2329 north for 9 miles to a junction with FSR 5603. Turn right and drive 2 miles to the trailhead parking area on the left.

Start the hike at the southern terminus and climb gradually through thin stands of young timber for 2 miles where you'll cross into the Mount Adams Wilderness Area. The forest transitions into old-growth pine, and near the 5.5-mile point, you'll find your first good views of the mountain as the trail nears Horseshoe Meadows. At the meadows, the trail bears sharply north as it skirts through heather meadows, staying just inside the vegetation zone—just above the trail, the vegetation gives way to the world of barren rock and ice that makes up the higher slopes of the mountain.

The trail maintains a fairly constant elevation, staying between 5,700 feet and 6,100 feet along the 10-mile stretch north of Horseshoe Meadows. Along the way, it passes lava beds, flower fields, and prominent geologic features such as The Bumper, The Hump, and Burnt Rock. The PCT turns away from the mountain at a trail junction 16 miles from the southern trailhead. While the PCT bears off to the left (north), the Highline Trail continues to traverse the upper flank of the mountain. Eventually, the Highline merges with the other high trails, and together with the PCT, these create a loop all the way around the mountain and are collectively known as the Round the Mountain Trail.

But that's a hike for another day (and another book). Staying left on the PCT, you'll begin a gradual descent through open forests and sun-filled clearings to the northern trailhead. About 20 miles from the southern end, the trail pierces a beautiful, ghostly silver forest. Huge, silver tree trunks stand amidst acres of huckleberry bushes, silent reminders of the power of forest fire—the fire flashed through, killing the trees, but it was moving so fast it didn't consume them.

Silver forest (i.e., barkless snags left standing after an old forest fire) near Killen Meadows

The trail skirts around a jumble of basalt on the western edge of a massive lava bed, the Muddy Fork Lava Bed, just at the wilderness boundary before the final 2 miles of gentle grade to the northern trailhead.

11 POTATO HILL

Distance: 3 miles round trip

Hiking time: 3 hours

High point: 5,387 feet

Elevation gain: 550 feet

Season: Mid- to late summer

Map: Green Trails Blue Lake, No. 334

Land manager: Mount Adams Ranger District

This is a good place for kids to come and explore. The PCT ducks the western face of Potato Hill, but the gentle cone can be climbed without much effort or difficulty. The scramble to the top is worth the effort as it brings wonderful views of Mount Adams and the volcanic landscape of the country north of the mountain. One of the most impressive sites is the sprawling Muddy Fork Lava Bed that seems to flow from the perfect cone of Red Butte (7,200 feet) on Mount Adams' northeast slope.

Potato Hill is centered on a north-south fault line that also runs under Mount Adams, and around 110,000 years ago, the mountain was formed when an eruption of basalt lava spewed out of the fissure along this fault line. The cinder cone that was left behind became Potato Hill.

To get there, from Packwood drive south on FSR 21 for 17 miles to a junction with FSR 2160. Turn left (east) onto FSR 2160 and continue 1.8 miles, crossing the Cispus River, and turn right (southwest) onto FSR 56. In 1.8 miles, leave FSR 56 by bearing left (south) onto FSR 2329. In 5.5 miles, turn left at a junction with FSR 5603 and drive 2 miles to the trailhead. To reach the trailhead from the south, follow the directions to the northern trailhead in Hike 10.

The PCT heads north from the trailhead with the perfect cone of Potato Hill in sight all the way. The trail is relatively level and well maintained, and the vegetation is mostly low trees and brush. The trail traverses around the base of Potato Hill and for 2 miles explores some pretty wildflower meadows before reaching an old dirt road.

Rather than hike to the road, though, explore the trail for a while, and then return to within .5 mile of the trailhead and pick a place to scamper off-trail and start up the gentle slope of the minivolcano. Be sure to stay on the western face of the peak because the entire eastern

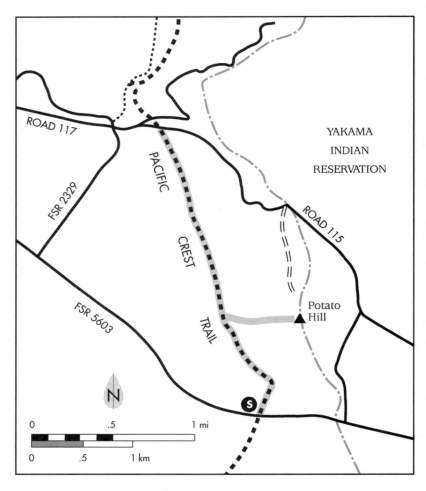

side is within the Yakama Indian Reservation and is off-limits to nontribal members. The boundary isn't marked, but by staying on the west and southwest sides, you'll remain on public land.

The sparse vegetation on the slopes makes climbing a warm experience when the sun is out, but it also means the top of the peak is always in sight—a quick glance up lets you know how much farther you've got to climb to get to the summit. If the 500-foot gain tires you, pull up for a breather and enjoy the wonderful views to the south and west. In addition to the beauty of Mount Adams, you'll see other prominent peaks, including Green Mountain and Hamilton Butte to the west.

Return to the trailhead by the same route.

Chipmunk looking for a handout on Potato Hill

12 COLEMAN WEEDPATCH

Distance: 9 miles round trip	
Hiking time: 5 hours	
High point: 5,700 feet	
Elevation gain: 1,900 feet	
Season: Mid- to late summer	
Map: Green Trails Walupt Lake, No. 335	
Land manager: Cowlitz Valley Ranger District	

Don't let the name scare you off—what some folks call weeds, hikers call wildflowers. The meadows visited by this trail are home to some of the finest blooming flowers in the country, and the views beyond aren't too bad either.

Look up from the brilliant floral display and you'll see Mount Adams on one side, Mount Rainier on another. The jagged crest of the Goat Rocks Peaks stretches to the north, and the deep blue waters of Walupt Lake lie below your feet, straight down the steep ridge wall.

To get there, from Packwood drive west on US 12 for 2 miles and turn left (south) onto FSR 21 (Johnson Creek Road). Continue about 19 miles on the sometimes-rough gravel road before turning left (east) onto FSR 2160, signed Walupt Lake Campground. The trailhead is about 3 miles down this road on the right.

Dense forest shelters the trail for the first mile and a half as it climbs gradually to the southwest, along the flank of a steep ridge. Views here are limited, but the cool forest is home to a variety of animals, from owls to elk, so pay attention to the surrounding woods and you might catch a glimpse of some of the beasties.

At 1.5 miles, the trail steepens considerably, but the climb is still modest—you'll gain a touch over 1,000 feet of elevation in the next 1.5 miles. During this stretch, the trees thin and the forest is broken by the occasional forest glade. The PCT is reached at 3 miles, and here is where the fun really begins. Turn north on the PCT and hike into the splendid country before you.

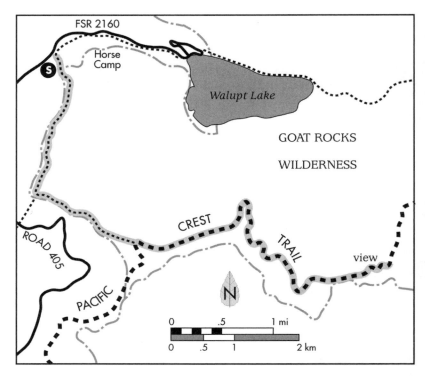

Coleman Weedpatch isn't all weeds; there are lots of views to be found, too.

Meadows, speckled with small groves of stunted subalpine evergreens, line the high route. Between the trees, acres of "weeds" sprout colorful blossoms throughout the summer—paintbrush, lupine, phlox, mountain daisies, heather, and columbine are a few of the plentiful flowers that grace these fields. Come autumn, when the blooms have died off, the meadows are colored by huckleberry bushes with their red autumn foliage and deep purple fruit (provided other hikers and bears haven't harvested the delicious berries first).

From the point where the PCT is reached, you'll hike about 1.5 miles through these open meadows with good views of Mount Adams and the smaller volcanoes along its base. The best views are found at 4.5 miles from the trailhead where the PCT crosses the top of a prominent knoll on the ridge crest. The top of this bluff offers an excellent place for lunch as you soak in the panoramic views—all around the slopes of the hill at your feet are wildflower meadows, and beyond are the snow-capped peaks of Mount Adams and the Goat Rocks Peaks.

The PCT descends into forest after leaving the top of the bluff on the ridge crest, so after lunch, turn back the way you came.

13 WALUPT LAKE LOOP

Distance: 12.5-mile loop

Hiking time: 8 hours (day hike or backpack)

High point: 5,800 feet

Elevation gain: 1,800 feet

Season: Mid- to late summer

Map: Green Trails Walupt Lake, No. 335

Land manager: Cowlitz Valley Ranger District

More a triangle than a loop, this route offers breathtaking views from the summit of Nannie Peak—just as you might expect from the site of a former fire lookout tower. There's more than views to this hike, though. You'll find wonderful wildflower meadows along the crest of Nannie Ridge, a clear, cold swimming experience in Sheep Lake, a walk along the spine of the Cascades on the PCT, and a cool forest hike in the Walupt Creek Valley.

The trail is short and gentle enough to enjoy as a long day hike, but the fine (though few) campsites at Sheep Lake, with their astounding views of Mount Adams (especially at sunset, when alpenglow sets the snowy

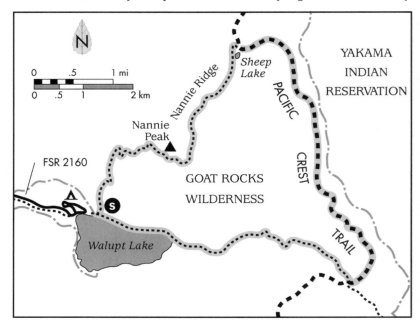

Lingering snow on Nannie Ridge

peak of Adams aflame with orange light), can be too tempting to pass up, as many backpackers can attest.

To get there, from Packwood drive west on US 12 for 2 miles and turn left (south) onto FSR 21 (Johnson Creek Road). Continue about 19 miles on the sometimes-rough gravel road before turning left (east) onto FSR 2160, signed Walupt Lake Campground. The trailhead is about 5 miles farther on at the end of this road near the pretty campground on the shores of Walupt Lake.

The loop can be hiked in either direction, but I prefer to do it clockwise—you'll find yourself facing more views this way as you hike. The Nannie Ridge Trail (No. 98) begins near the eastern end of the campground, climbing north through dense pine forests for more than 1 mile, crossing a couple of shallow creeks (often dry late in the year), and gradually gaining elevation. As the trail nears the 1.5-mile point, the forests begin to open with spacious clearings scattered throughout. Here's where the fun begins. Hit the trail in late August and you'll find these clearings a deep shape of purple, provided you get there before the other hikers and the bears. Huckleberries the size of marbles and sweeter than honey cover the lower slopes of Nannie Peak. (There are so many here, I don't mind sharing this information.)

The trail continually steepens over the next mile, and deep ruts cut many of the switchbacks—be sure to stay on the true trail and don't use the shortcuts or the braided sections of trail. (Braided trails are sections where hikers and horses have created multiple, parallel trails that weave back and forth together, forming a broad network of trails instead of one simple path.)

At 3 miles, the trail tops the ridge crest just below the summit of Nannie Peak. A short, .5-mile way-trail leads to the summit of the peak, and it is well worth the effort to scramble up this boot-beaten path to enjoy the outstanding views and wonderful mountaintop meadows. The views are dominated by three big southern volcanoes—Mount Rainier to the north, Mount Adams to the south, and Mount St. Helens to the southwest—but the jagged crests of the Goat Rocks Peaks to the northeast are also not to be missed.

The trail continues east from Nannie Peak, following just below the crest of Nannie Ridge—the trail drops several hundred feet below the ridge for a while in order to avoid some towering cliffs. At 4.4 miles, you'll find Sheep Lake at the junction with the PCT. The best campsite is on the knoll to the south of the lake where you'll enjoy evening views of alpenglow on Mount Adams.

To complete the loop, turn south on the PCT and hike along meadows and ponds. If you are backpacking, note that if Sheep Lake fills up with campers, some fine sites are located along the headwaters of Walupt Creek just .5 mile down the PCT from the lake.

As the PCT weaves past a cluster of small ponds 5 miles south of Sheep Lake, turn right onto the Walupt Creek Trail. The trail follows the southern fork of the creek about 4.5 miles back to the trailhead at Walupt Lake.

14 CISPUS PASS LOOP

Distance: 18-mile loop	
Hiking time: 2 days	
High point: 6,400 feet	
Elevation gain: 2,400 feet	
Season: Late summer to early autumn	
Maps: Green Trails Blue Lake, No. 334, and Walupt Lake, No. 335	
Land manager: Cowlitz Valley Ranger District, Packwood Office	

This hike can be done as a loop, but it is just as enjoyable as an out-and-back trip to the pass. The route climbs to a 6,400-foot pass on the flank of

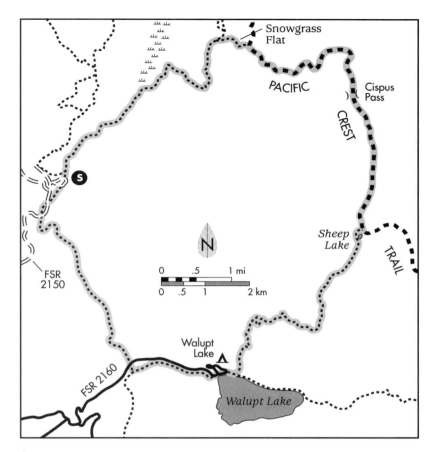

glacier-laden Gilbert Peak, slicing through forest, meadows, and huckle-berry thickets along the way.

The trail climbs through some of the most spectacular wildflower meadows in the state and presents some of the most wonderful views you could imagine. Volcanoes loom on all sides: Mount Rainier, Mount Adams, Mount St. Helens, and on clear days, even Mount Hood can be seen far to the south. But it's not just the big snow-cap cones that are seen. Lesser volcanoes—perfectly formed cinder cones—can be seen scattered throughout the southern Cascades, in addition to the ancient volcanic peaks of the Goat Rocks. The peaks along the Goat Rocks Crest are the last remaining bits of an ancient volcano that formed and collapsed long before the current peaks poked up.

To get there, from Packwood drive west on US 12 for 2 miles and turn

Horseback riders (and a dog) on the PCT near Cispus Pass

left (south) onto FSR 21 (Johnson Creek FSR). Continue about 15.5 miles on the sometimes-rough gravel road before turning left (east) onto FSR 2150, signed Chambers Lake Campground. In 3 miles, turn right onto FSR 040, and shortly, turn right again on FSR 405. Drive to the trailhead (signed Berry Patch) at the road end, about 20 miles from Highway 12.

A short spur trail leads west from the trailhead, and in less than .25 mile, it joins the Snowgrass Flat Trail (No. 96). The initial going is in heavy forest cover, and near the 2-mile mark, the trail crosses Goat Creek and swings into a cedar swamp. This swamp is one of the reasons I recommend early autumn as the prime hiking season. By waiting until September to enjoy this hike, you'll find the high pass snow-free and the swamp will be mostly bug-free—hike in August and there will likely be snowfields at the pass and swarms of blood-hungry mosquitoes in the swamp. Of course, the marsh is a mere .25-mile long, so if you do come here in the summer months, a bit of bug-dope and a fast pace will protect you from the worst of the bugs.

Once past the wetlands, the trail climbs 1,100 feet in the next 2 miles to reach the lower meadows of Snowgrass Flat at 4.1 miles. Here you'll find a trail junction. Turn right onto Bypass Trail, and hike .5 mile southwest along the edge of the Snowgrass meadows to a 6,100-foot junction with the PCT. Turn right onto the PCT, and head south through spectacular subalpine environments. The trail traverses the rocky slope of the upper Cispus River Basin, and 2 miles after joining the PCT, you'll cross Cispus Pass on the western flank of Gilbert Peak. The last .5 mile before the pass climbs along a north-facing slope, which often has lingering snowfields on it well into August.

Cispus Pass, at 6.6 miles from the trailhead, is a good turnaround point for day hikers. The views here are outstanding. Looking south from the pass, Mount Adams dominates the skyline. Looking north, Mount Rainier towers on the horizon. In either direction, heather and flower-filled meadows sprawl underfoot.

To complete the loop, cross the pass and descend into the Klickitat River Basin. The trail skirts along the upper basin for 1 mile before topping out onto a saddle in the ridge and then crossing over to the Nannie Creek Basin. A gradual descent through meadows and broken forest leads to a junction with the Nannie Ridge Trail near Sheep Lake in another mile, 8.6 miles from the trailhead. Sheep Lake makes a fine campsite, but if it is full, additional camps can be found .5 mile south of the lake on the PCT near a crossing with the North Fork of Walupt Creek.

From Sheep Lake, descend the Nannie Ridge Trail (see Hike 13) to Walupt Lake. Walking 1.5 miles down the Walupt Lake access road leads to a Coleman Weedpatch Trailhead. Find the small trail on the north side of the road at the trail, and follow it 3.5 miles back to the trailhead. This trail crosses several old clearcuts and logging roads, so you might want to avoid this unsightly section of trail. To do so, simply arrange to have a second vehicle waiting at Walupt Lake.

15 GOAT LAKE LOOP AND BASECAMP

Distance: 13-mile loop

Hiking time: 8 hours (day hike, 2-day backpack, or multi-day basecamp hiking)

High point: 6,500 feet

Elevation gain: 1,900 feet

Season: Late summer to early autumn

Maps: Green Trails White Pass, No. 303; Blue Lake, No. 334; and Walupt Lake, No. 335

Land manager: Cowlitz Valley Ranger District

The Goat Lake Loop just touches the PCT, but it provides a wonderful loop to one of the most scenic points on the trail. More importantly, if

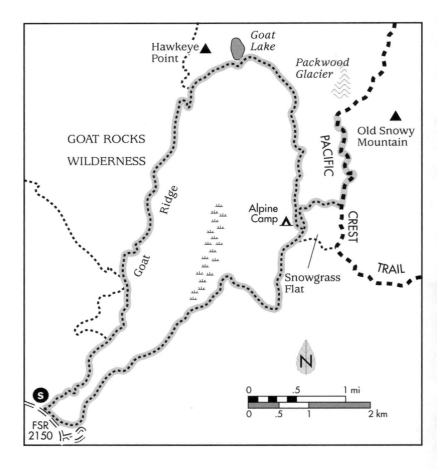

you are backpacking, the loop provides locations where you can set up a high camp and enjoy long day hikes to the north and south along the PCT. Camp at Goat Lake—high above timberline—and enjoy hiking on the crest trail, exploring miles of subalpine meadows and high mountain passes.

To get there, from Packwood drive west on US 12 for 2 miles and turn left (south) onto FSR 21 (Johnson Creek Road). Continue about 15.5 miles on the sometimes-rough gravel road before turning left (east) onto FSR 2150, signed Chambers Lake Campground. In 3.5 miles, turn right onto a short dirt road that leads into the trailhead parking area, just above Chambers Lake Campground.

To hike the loop clockwise, start up the Goat Ridge Trail (No. 95) as it climbs the snout of Goat Ridge. The first 1.5 miles pierce old pine and fir forests. The widely spaced trees create an open canopy that allows lots of sunshine to reach the forest floor, and taking advantage of that plentiful light is a sprawling mass of huckleberry bushes. The berries aren't as big and juicy as some found in more open meadows, but the fruit offers a tasty treat to hikers plodding up the steep trail.

A small side trail branches off to the left at 1.5 miles—this is merely a scenic alternative that loops out around the steep west slope of Goat Ridge while the main trail hugs the meadow-dotted east side of the ridge. Just over .5 mile down the main trail, the secondary trail rejoins it. (At 1.1 miles long, the alternative trail is more than 1 mile longer than the main route.)

Looking southwest toward Snowgrass Flat from Goat Lake

Just after the first trail junction, the forest begins to open up, first with small forest glades scattered along the ridge, and then finally the trees give way to broad, rolling meadows as the trail crosses under a large talus slope at 2.5 miles. Marmots thrive in this rocky slope, and so do predators—it was here that I encountered the largest coyote I've ever seen, hunting the whistling marmots.

Above this point, the trail climbs steeply into the flower-filled meadows. The views gradually improve as you ascend until, at 3.8 miles, the trail crosses over Goat Ridge in a deep saddle under Hawkeye Point. This ridge provides outstanding views west into the wildflower wonderland of Jordan Basin to the west and Goat Creek Basin to the east. Far beyond, look out over the gray-green forests of the Cispus River Valley to the west.

From the ridge crossing, the trail traverses around the upper basin of Goat Creek to reach Goat Lake at 5 miles. A few campsites are situated along the shores of the intensely cold lake. The lake is nestled in a north-face rocky cirque and frequently has an ice shelf covering a portion of the water year-round.

To access the PCT from Goat Lake, continue southeast as the trail completes the traverse around the head of Goat Creek Basin, and at 7 miles, reach Alpine Camp in the meadows above Snowgrass Flat. Camping is prohibited in the flats, but excellent tent sites can be found in Alpine Camp.

From Alpine Camp, turn east and hike a small trail .5 mile to join the PCT and enjoy the wonderful views of Gilbert Peak to the southeast and Old Snowy Mountain to the north. Far to the south, Mount Adams punctuates the skyline.

If you are a basecamper staying at Alpine Camp (or at Goat Lake), turn north on the PCT and head north about 2 miles to Old Snowy. The trail crosses the flank of the mountain at the 7,600-foot level, traversing the upper section of Packwood Glacier. This is the highest section of the PCT in Washington.

If you turn south on the PCT from the Alpine Camp junction, you will cross Cispus Pass in 2.5 miles for excellent views of the Klickitat Basin and Klickton Ridge to the east in the Yakama Indian Reservation.

To close the loop, from Alpine Camp descend through Snowgrass Flat and drop down to the Berry Patch Trailhead in 4 miles, and then take the .5-mile connecting trail to the Goat Ridge Trailhead where you started.

16 EGG BUTTE VIA PACKWOOD LAKE

Distance: 27 miles round trip
Hiking time: 2 to 3 days
High point: 6,700 feet
Elevation gain: 5,300 feet
Season: late summer to early autumn
Maps: Green Trails Packwood, No. 302 and White Pass, No. 303
Land manager: Cowlitz Valley Ranger District

It's a long approach hike to reach the PCT, but it's worth the effort. Not only because the section you'll encounter is so spectacular, but also because the trail leading to the PCT is wonderfully scenic, remarkably quiet, and seldom used.

This route provides an experience in a wide variety of ecosystems, from deep river-valley forests to low-elevation lakes, to alpine and subalpine meadows, to glacier-covered peaks.

The trail leads past sprawling Packwood Lake with its popular campgrounds and up the forest-lined valley of Lake Creek before climbing steeply to the PCT at Elk Pass on the flank of Egg Butte.

To get there, from Packwood follow US 12 to the east end of town

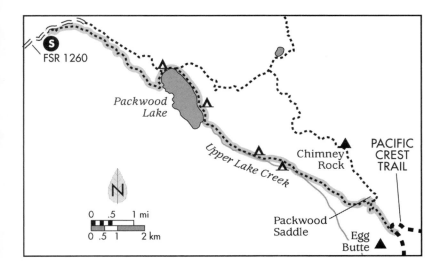

and turn southeast onto FSR 1260 (found right next to the USFS Packwood Ranger Station). Continue southeast on FSR 1260 for 6 miles to the trailhead parking lot.

The Packwood Lake Trail (No. 78) weaves through old second-growth forests for 4 miles, with views limited to the trees around you. As the trail nears the lake, you'll find peak-a-boo views up the valley to the jagged crest of Goat Rocks. At 4.6 miles, the trail reaches an old ranger station at the end of the lake (2,900 feet). A wide, wooden bridge crosses the outlet stream, and the trail passes by the campground just beyond the bridge. The trail continues around the end of the lake and heads east along the north side of the mile-long lake.

For the next 5 miles, the trail follows Lake Creek up-valley, gaining just 300 feet in that distance. Plenty of small campsites are scattered along the creek for those who prefer to avoid the crowded campground at the mouth of the lake.

The trail climbs away from the creek around the 10-mile point, heading steeply up the valley wall to Packwood Saddle at 12 miles (elevation

5,500 feet). The saddle sits nestled between Chimney Rock and Egg Butte, with wonderful views of both peaks. But it's Old Snowy Mountain behind Egg Butte that dominates the vistas. The trail heads toward the small knob of Egg Butte (6,035 foot), and in 1.5 miles, the trail ends at a junction with the PCT at Elk Pass.

The view from the pass looks west to an oval knob known as Egg Butte and south to the glacier-covered slopes of Old Snowy Mountain. Scramble around these rocky slopes at your leisure before returning to the Packwood Lake Basin.

Moonrise over the ridge near Egg Butte

17 NORTH TIETON RIVER LOOP

Distance: 11.5-mile loop
Hiking time: 7 hours (day hike or backpack)
High point: 5,800 feet
Elevation gain: 2,500 feet
Season: July to October
Map: Green Trails White Pass, No. 303
Land manager: Naches Ranger District

Deep pine forests dominate this route, offering an experience in dry-side ecosystems. The trail weaves around massive orange-tinted ponderosa pines and through fragrant spruce groves. Beavers and otters swim in the river below the trail, and owls, hawks, and eagles soar in the air overhead. Huge elk, mule deer, and black bear wander the hillsides around the trail, and snakes, coyotes, and cougars prowl the brush between the trees.

Although river-valley clearings, hillside forests, and high alpine meadows can be found on this short, scenic loop, very few people hike this route.

To get there, from White Pass drive east on US 12 to Rimrock Lake and turn south onto Clear Lake Road (FSR 1200). Continue about 3 miles, contouring around the west end of Clear Lake, before turning south onto

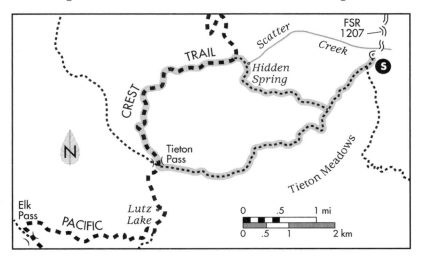

Wildflowers near the head of the North Tieton River Trail at its junction with the PCT

FSR 1207 (North Fork Tieton River Road). Drive south on Road 1207 to the trailhead at the road end.

From the riverside trailhead, the trail climbs gradually away from the water, gaining 600 feet in 1.2 miles to reach a trail junction. For the easiest climbing, stay left on the main trail (No. 1118) as it continues to parallel the river while gradually ascending the valley wall. The trail crosses several small creeks, but it stays mostly in pine forest for the next 3 miles, with few views beyond the pine trunks. Early-season hikers may enjoy blooming beargrass and some patches of crimson columbine, but by midsummer it's a dry forest devoid of color beyond the ever-present greens and browns.

The scenery changes as the trail turns steeper until, at 4.9 miles, the trail reaches the PCT at Tieton Pass, elevation 4,800 feet. Turn north, and follow the PCT through forest glades and gardens of wildflowers while still gaining elevation. Three miles north, you'll be 1,000 feet higher (elevation 5,800 feet) and will have crossed some pretty meadows with wonderful views of Tieton Peak to the south.

At that point, near Hidden Spring—some 8 miles from the trailhead—leave the PCT and start a steep descent along Trail No. 1117 back to the Tieton River Valley. This trail drops 2,000 feet in 2.5 miles. Great views are found on the first .5 mile, but after that the trail plunges into tree-lined switchbacks with few views. The trail ends at a junction with the North Tieton River Trail (No. 1118). Turn left, and retrace your steps over the 1.2 miles to the trailhead.

18 SHOE LAKE

Distance: 14 miles round trip

Hiking time: 8 hours (day hike—no camping allowed at lake)

High point: 6,600 feet

Elevation gain: 2,200 feet

Season: July through October

Map: Green Trails White Pass, No. 303

Land manager: Naches Ranger District

It's unfortunate that prior abuses of the Shoe Lake Basin have forced the area to be closed to camping, but the lake—and the hike to it—is pretty enough that a long day hike to the area is well worth the effort. Shoe Lake was overrun by campers in the 1980s, and the fragile meadows around the pond were crisscrossed with social trails and dotted with bare-earth tent sites. In the years since, camping has been prohibited and the vegetation has slowly recovered, although faint trails still show through the wildflowers.

The trail to the lake is in great shape, though. The route along Hogback Mountain is a classic example of what most folks think of when they hear Pacific "Crest" Trail—a faint footpath through alpine meadows hugging the side of a knife-edged ridge.

To get there, drive US 12 to White Pass. The PCT South Trailhead is located just east of the ski area on the south side of the highway.

Shoe Lake as seen from the PCT above

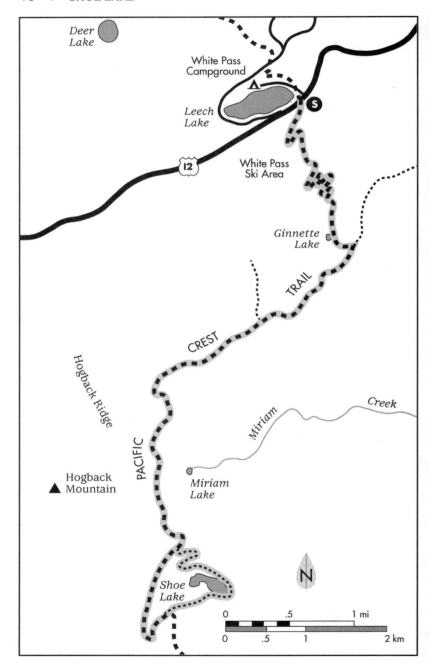

The trail angles southeast for the first 2.5 miles, skirting the edge of the White Pass Ski Area. This initial section climbs modestly through open pine forests, gaining 1,000 feet in those 2.5 miles, to a junction with the Three Peaks Trail. The route bears west and the forest opens even more as the trail weaves between sun-dappled woods and sun-filled meadows. At 3.5 miles, a short spur trail leads north to the top of the ski lifts. The PCT, though, continues southwest along the east flank of Hogback Mountain.

This remnant of the once-great Goat Rocks Volcano is a jagged peak with long, knife-sharp ridges leading north and south from the summit. The trail hugs the southern ridge, contouring along the 6,400-foot level. A few wildflowers struggle for survival on this steep slope, but mostly the trail slides across scree slopes and pika-playgrounds on the curving ridge wall. At just over 6 miles from the trail, the PCT crosses a narrow shoulder of the mountain at 6,600 feet. Pause here to soak up the incredible views before you—the horseshoe-shaped Shoe Lake lies 400 feet below, while far beyond the lake to the southeast is the cliff-lined Pinegrass Ridge.

From the ridge top, it's another .5 mile down to the lakeshore, and then there's a .5-mile trail around the lake to explore. Wildflower meadows surround the lake, with a small grove of shady evergreens on the peninsula in the center of the lake's horseshoe. If you want to camp nearby, return to the PCT and continue south about 1 mile to Hidden Spring Camp. Return the way you came.

19 GOAT ROCKS THRU HIKE

Distance: 30 miles one-way	
Hiking time: 3 to 4 days	
High point: 7,600 feet	
Elevation gain: 5,300 feet	
Season: Late summer to early autumn	
Maps: Green Trails White Pass, No. 303, and Walupt Lake, No. 335	
Land manager: Cowlitz Valley Ranger District	

The peaks along the spine of the Goat Rocks look impressive today, but at one point they were mere bumps along the flank of a volcano the size of Mount Rainier. A series of eruptions more than a million years ago started the long process of decimating the volcano. Those eruptions, and natural

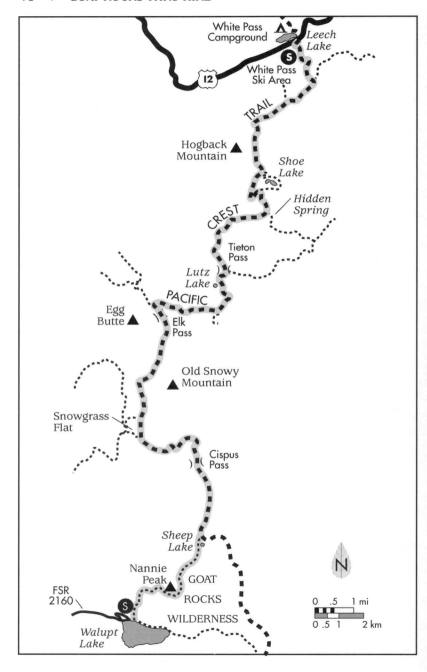

erosion, brought the great cone down, leaving the jagged series of mountains that comprise the Goat Rocks Peaks today. The PCT follows this spine, crossing through some of the most pristine wilderness in Washington. It is in the Goat Rocks that the PCT ascends to its highest point in Washington—7,600 feet on Old Snowy Mountain—and it is here that you will find some of the most solitary traveling on the PCT. Because of its distance from major urban centers, and the length of the trails leading into the heart of the wilderness, the Goat Rocks attract relatively few day hikers. If you backpack this trail, generally you will find that you can enjoy quiet wilderness camps without worrying about neighbors.

To get to the northern trailhead, drive US 12 to the summit of White Pass. The PCT trailhead parking area is found on the south side of the highway, about 1 mile east of the ski area. To get to the southern trailhead, follow the directions to Walupt Lake Loop (Hike 13).

From White Pass, head south along the PCT as it climbs through the thin second-growth forest just east of the ski area. The first 2.5 miles climb gently, gaining just 1,000 feet. At a junction with the Three Peaks Trail on the left, the PCT veers west, and in another mile, it passes the top of the ski area. (A short trail on the right leads .25 mile north to the ski lifts.)

From here, the trail follows the wilderness boundary south along the eastern flank of Hogback Mountain, crosses a sharp-edged shoulder of the mountain at 6,600 feet, and passes Shoe Lake at 7 miles. In order to let the area recover from overuse, camping is prohibited in the Shoe Lake Basin, but just 1 mile farther on, a few campsites are located near Hidden Spring.

The springs are in cool pine forests, and for the next few miles, you will stay in the trees until the path crosses Tieton Pass (4,800 feet) at 11 miles. The pass is the scene of a four-way intersection as the North Fork Tieton River Trail comes in from the east and the Cowlitz River Trail enters from the west. The PCT continues south, climbing gradually past Lutz Lake to another trail junction at 13 miles. The trail on the left descends gradually into McCall Basin and ends in 1 mile near a pretty waterfall.

From this junction, the PCT turns west and climbs steeply to Elk Pass, where it turns south once more and traverses around Egg Butte to reach the Packwood Glacier on Old Snowy Mountain. This stretch of the trail stays well above the vegetation zone, seldom dipping below 7,000 feet in the next few miles.

View along the PCT near the Walupt Creek Trail junction

From Old Snowy, the trail drops past Snowgrass Flat and Cispus Pass before reaching Sheep Lake at the eastern end of Nannie Ridge at 25 miles. Leave the PCT here and follow Nannie Ridge west to the Walupt Lake Trailhead.

20 SAND LAKE

Distance: 6 miles round trip	
Hiking time: 4 hours	
High point: 5,300 feet	
Elevation gain: 900 feet	
Season: Early summer to late autumn	
Map: Green Trails White Pass, No. 303	
Land manager: Naches Ranger District	

Bring the kids on this excursion—it's a great introduction to the PCT for youngsters. The elevation gain is minimal, the scenery is pretty, and the lake at the end of the hike offers an idyllic swimming experience. Although wilderness lakes stay ice cold throughout the summer, Sand Lake is just shallow enough for the sun to warm it to a comfortable temperature for cooling off during a hot summer hike. The smooth, sandy bottom is a comfort to boot-tired feet, too.

A slew of lakes in the southern half of the William O. Douglas Wilderness Area are worth visiting, and Sand Lake is the second you'll pass on this trip. Deer Lake is the first you'll encounter, and between them you'll find acres of wildflower meadows and cool stands of pine forests.

To get there, drive US 12 to White Pass. The PCT North Trailhead is found just east of the Ski Area at White Pass Campground. Turn onto a poorly marked road on the east end of Leech Lake and drive a few hundred yards to the trailhead, which is situated between the horse camp and the car campground.

The trail enters the forest at the trailhead and stays under cover of trees for most of its length. The steepest climbing of the hike occurs during the first mile of trail, but don't fret—you'll gain just 400 feet in that mile. From there, the trail levels considerably and the forest thins out, allowing lots of sunlight to filter down to the brush covering the forest floor. That's a blessing because the sunshine sweetens the purple fruit that grows on that brush. Huckleberries! These forest berries are neither as thick nor as big as those found in the open clearings and meadows throughout the wilderness, but they are delicious nonetheless. The fruit is plentiful enough to keep young hikers happy as they tread up the trail, even if it does throw you off your stride. (Pick, step, pick, pick, step, pick, pick, pick, step!)

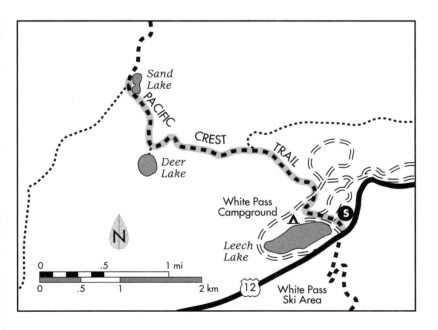

The PCT heads north under more than three feet of water, thanks to flooded Sand Lake.

The PCT veers west at 1.3 miles, just before reaching a junction with a small side trail on the right leading to Dog Lake. Stay on the main track and in another mile reach a second spur trail, this time on the left. Take a few minutes to hike the 100 yards down this trail to Deer Lake, a forest-lined lake holding a good population of catchable (and keepable) trout, so bring along fishing rods for you and the youngsters. The lake is frequently stocked with cutthroat, and brook trout reside here also.

If you aren't fishing, jump back onto the PCT and continue north on the now-level path for another mile or so to Sand Lake. This last mile crosses several broad meadows (in early summer, the meadows are more like marshes), and it offers the best chance of seeing big critters such as deer and elk. Meadows push right up against Sand Lake, although stands of timber do too. The lake is actually a catch basin for runoff from melting snow. No permanent stream runs into the lake or out of it. As snow melts, the water rolls into the lake basin, where it gathers, swelling the lake in early summer. After most of the snow has melted off, the lake waters slowly recede as some evaporates and some perks down through the porous volcanic soil.

Ideally, you'll visit here in late July to early August, when the waters are low enough to be off the lakeside trail but still high enough to be clear and cool. If you want to spend the night (it's a great destination for the kids' first backpacking trip), you will find plenty of high, grassy campsites around the lake basin. Just be sure to stay well back from the water so as not to intrude on the scenery and to protect the lake itself.

Return to the trailhead by the same route.

21 DUMBBELL LAKE LOOP

Distance: 15-mile loop
Hiking time: 7 hours (day hike or backpack)
High point: 5,600 feet
Elevation gain: 1,200 feet
Season: Early summer to late autumn
Map: Green Trails White Pass, No. 303
Land manager: Naches Ranger District

Sweeping out around Cramer Mountain and back under the shadow of conical Spiral Butte, this loop explores the forests, meadows, lakes, and mountains of the southwestern section of the William O. Douglas Wilderness Area. Even though you're hiking the PCT, it's the lakes and meadows that make this trip special, not the peaks and high ridges. Indeed, there are no high ridges on this leg of the "Crest."

The loop might seem a little long for a day hike, but because the route is relatively flat and the trail is generally well maintained you can keep up a good pace throughout the route. The recommended way to enjoy this trip, though, is as an overnight backpacking trip, especially if you are an angler. Dumbbell Lake supports a strong population of cutthroat and eastern brook trout.

Nonanglers will also enjoy camping at Dumbbell because of the plentiful scenery and the nice scramble route to the tree-free top of Cramer Mountain.

To get there, drive US 12 to White Pass. The PCT North Trailhead is found just east of the Ski Area at White Pass Campground. Turn onto a poorly marked road on the east end of Leech Lake and drive a few hundred yards to the trailhead, which is situated between the horse camp and the car campground.

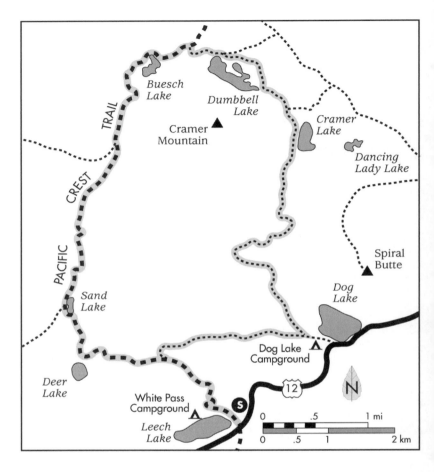

Head up the trail as it climbs gradually through the pine forest, passing Deer Lake at around the 2.5-mile mark and Sand Lake around the 3-mile point. Many day hikers stop at Sand Lake, and it's worth pausing for a snack break here to enjoy the pretty, sandy-bottomed lake. If the day is hot, you might even consider a dip in the refreshingly cool waters before pushing on.

Beyond Sand Lake the trail rolls north, climbing a meager 400 feet in the next 2 miles. Along this section, the country surrounding the trail transitions from meadow to forest, and back to meadow. Interspersed throughout is a slew of tiny unnamed ponds and potholes—some are big enough to be clear and cold, others are tiny and good for little besides breeding mosquitoes. Note: If you are hiking in the early summer, bring plenty of good bug repellent! The meadows and forest clearings offer frequent views of Mount Adams and the Goat Rock Peaks to the south, Mount Rainier to the northwest, and Spiral Butte to the east.

Snow lingers along the PCT near Dumbbell Lake.

At 6 miles from the trailhead, the trail sweeps east around Buesch Lake, and in another .5 mile, it reaches a junction with Trail No. 56 to Dumbbell Lake. Take this right-hand trail, and in .5 mile, you'll reach the wide, deep waters of Dumbbell. Find an open campsite around the rocky shores of this lake, or continue along the trail for another mile to camp at Cramer Lake. Scramblers can find a route to the top of Cramer Mountain (5,992 feet) from either lake—just push through the brush on the lower flank of the mountain, and you'll have an easy climb on the treeless upper slopes. From the top of Cramer, you'll find fabulous views of the entire William O. Douglas Wilderness Area, as well as the Goat Rocks Wilderness Area, Mount Adams, and Mount Rainier.

To close the loop, continue south on Trail No. 56 from Cramer Lake. The trail descends into the trees, crosses the North Fork of Clear Creek, and at about 4.5 miles south of Cramer Lake, the trail nears Dog Lake. Look for a faint trail (Trail No. 1107) on the right leading due west. This trail connects with the PCT just 1.2 miles north of the trailhead.

Note: Trail No. 1107 is occasionally brushy and overgrown. (Trail maintenance schedules are sometimes haphazard.) If the path is difficult to find, merely head out to Dog Lake and hike 1.5 miles west along US 12 back to the trailhead at Leech Lake.

22 TUMAC MOUNTAIN RAMBLE

Distance: 24 to 30 miles round trip	
Hiking time: 2 to 4 days	
High point: 6,340 feet	
Elevation gain: 1,900 feet	
Season: Early summer to late autumn	
Map: Green Trails White Pass, No. 303	
Land manager: Naches Ranger District	

Don't think of this as a loop hike—it's more like a pretzel. The network of trails in the southern half of the William O. Douglas Wilderness Area makes plotting a course a matter of simply deciding how far you want to hike and then finding the necessary connecting trails to create a loop of that length.

The region not only has plenty of trails to offer, but it has a plethora

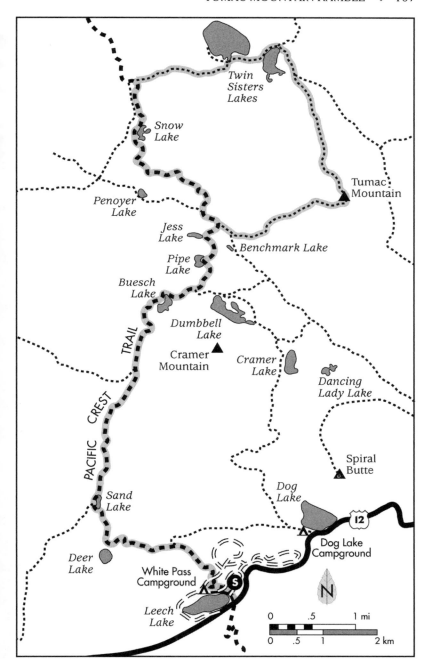

of terrain to explore as well. The one feature that all the routes have in common is an abundance of water. Lakes large and small dot this wilderness. Looking at a map of the southern section of the William O. Douglas Wilderness Area, you might think the cartographer spilled a bottle of blue ink. Blue dots are sprinkled liberally over the map, illustrating the more than 100 charted lakes, ponds, potholes, puddles, and tarns found in the region. That's good news for anglers, bad news for those of us prone to attracting mosquitoes.

But there is more to the trails than water. A number of buttes and mountains tower over the sprawling meadows and forestlands. Most of these are volcanic in nature, as is apparent from their perfect cone shapes and ashy coverings. A few of the peaks have trails to the top, but most are bare, rocky knobs that can be easily scrambled up for stunning views of the South Cascades.

This route takes advantage of the best of the lakes, meadows, and mountains of the region.

To get there, drive US 12 to White Pass. The PCT North Trailhead is found just east of the Ski Area at White Pass Campground. Turn onto a poorly marked road on the east end of Leech Lake and drive a few hundred yards to the trailhead, which is situated between the horse camp and the car campground.

Follow the PCT north as if heading to Dumbbell Lake (Hike No. 21), passing Deer and Sand Lakes before arriving at Buesch Lake at the 6-mile mark. Continue north on the PCT from Buesch for another 4.5 miles, following a meandering path through a network of lakes and puddles (the largest of which is Pipe Lake, passed in the first mile of this leg). Along the way, you'll encounter two trail junctions—at the first junction, about 1.3 miles from Buesch, stay left as the Tumac Mountain Trail (No. 44) veers east, and .25 mile past that, stay right at the second junction where the Penoyer Lake Trail (again, No. 44) heads west.

From Buesch Lake north, the PCT stays near the 5,000-foot elevation, climbing and dipping no more than 200 feet in 4 miles. Then at 11 miles from the trailhead, leave the PCT by hiking east on the Twin Sisters Trail (No. 980). This trail crosses the narrow strip of land between the large Twin Sisters Lakes in 1.5 miles from the PCT. Fine campsites are all around these two lakes. Less than .5 mile farther along the path, you'll encounter

Hikers bushwhacking along the flank of Tumac Mountain

another trail junction. Trail No. 980 slants north to follow Deep Creek away from Twin Sisters; take the right fork and head south on Trail No. 44 toward Tumac Mountain.

In .5 mile, near the lower end of Little Twin Sister Lake, there's yet another junction. Stay right on Trail No. 44, unless you are looking for a longer hike. Trail No. 1105A heads east into appropriately named Mosquito Valley and down to Blankenship Lakes before turning back north to reconnect with No. 44. This side loop adds 4 miles to the overall trip distance.

Staying on Trail No. 44, though, will lead you 1 mile south through sweeping meadows just south of the Twin Sisters Lakes where the trail begins a gentle approach to Tumac Mountain. Another mile of steep climbing gets you to the top of Tumac (6,340 feet). This cinder-cone volcano provides awesome views of the lake country you just crossed.

Leaving the summit, you'll drop down the southern face and veer west, still on Trail No. 44, reaching the PCT near Jess Lake in just 2 miles. (Another loop can be added using the Dumbbell Lake Loop described in Hike 21.) At this point, you'll have covered no less than 17 miles since leaving the trailhead (more if you explored other loop options). It's now a simple matter of returning 6.5 miles south on the PCT back to the trailhead.

23 TIPSOO LAKE TO AMERICAN RIDGE

Distance:	13 miles round trip
Hiking time:	6 hours (day hike or backpack)
High point:	5,800 feet
Elevation gain:	700-foot loss
Season:	August when the flowers are blooming or September when the berries are ripe
Maps:	Green Trails Mount Rainier East, No. 270, and Bumping Lake No. 271
Land manager:	Naches Ranger District

The short stretch of the PCT rolling along the boundary between Mount Rainier National Park and the William O. Douglas Wilderness Area offers a total sensory experience. Hike south from Tipsoo Lake to the western end of American Ridge and you'll find wonderful vistas spread before

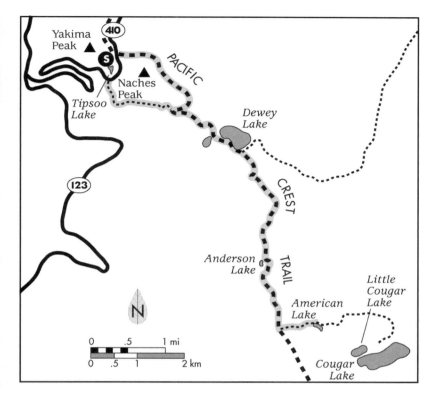

your eyes—Mount Rainier towers above a rainbow array of wildflower blooms. The flowers fill the air with the fragrant perfume of the wilderness, drifting around the trail on the gentle breezes wafting up from the dry canyons on the east slope of the Cascades. Those same winds provide a cool caress for overheated hikers trekking along the crest. Listen to the marmots whistle at your passing as you hike along the rocky slopes near the shores of Dewey and American Lakes.

To get there, drive east from Enumclaw on SR 410 to the summit of Chinook Pass. Park on the north side of the highway, in the Lake Tipsoo Parking Area. Cross to the south side of the highway to find the start of the trail.

Climb the grassy hillside on the south side of the highway, and follow it as it climbs southeast for .5 mile. This small connector trail slices through a few small stands of trees but generally rolls through broad meadows of alpine wildflowers. To the west, Mount Rainier fills the horizon. The trail climbs gradually for the first .5 mile and then levels out until it reaches a trail junction at 1.5 miles. This is where you meet the true PCT. Turn left for a 1.5-mile hike north to SR 410—the trail meets the highway .5 mile east of Lake Tipsoo. For an extended outing, turn right and begin a moderately steep descent, dropping some 600 feet in 1.3 miles.

The trail drops through a series of gentle switchbacks, passing through old, sun-dappled pine and fir forest, to reach a small forest clearing on the northwest shore of Dewey Lake. This broad, trout-filled lake is a great backpacking destination for families—the 3-mile hike (one way) is gentle, and the lake is a great place to swim, fish, or just relax and enjoy the scenery.

Beyond Dewey Lake, the PCT rolls nearly due south and brings you into the country that was loved so dearly by the late William O. Douglas—the Yakima native who grew up to become a U.S. Supreme Court Justice (served 1939-75). Douglas was a sickly child—he nearly died of infantile paralysis—but he overcame his illness by trudging up and down the dry mountains west of Yakima. As his body grew stronger, so did his love of this pristine area, and a lifelong bond was formed. The wilderness that bears his name sprawls over the east slope of the Cascades all the way up to the PCT.

From the southeast end of Dewey Lake, the trail rolls gently south, cutting through huge expanses of huckleberry meadows—excellent places to savor the essence of pine forest. Be aware that berry-hungry bears also like to gobble the juicy fruit.

Camp set up near American Lake

Douglas himself made this trek, enjoying the succulent berries along the way. His written account of it—the autobiographical *Of Men and Mountains*—describes a hike along this stretch of the crest trail that he made as a young boy. Just north of American Ridge, near Anderson Lake at the head of Deer Creek, Douglas and his brother hiked into a wide meadow on an open hillside on the eastern slope of the crest (where the PCT now lies).

"The hillside was filled with patches of low-bush huckleberries that were heavy with ripe fruit. We dropped our packs and sat on the ground and once more ate our fill. Some of the berries were twice as big as peas. We tossed them down by the handful, hungry for the sugar that sunlight had stored in them." (*Of Men and Mountains* [San Francisco: Chronicle Books, 1990], p. 72.)

This enormous patch of huckleberries is just as rich in fruit today, and you can eat your fill before hiking on to Anderson Lake at 4.4 miles. The trail climbs gently for the next mile, rolling along the western flank of a small, unnamed peak (5,982 feet) before reaching the junction with the American Ridge Trail at 5.8 miles. For a good campsite, hike east for .75 mile on the American Ridge Trail to American Lake, where you'll enjoy more huckleberry fields and scenery that includes a rocky pinnacle to the south and the deep valley of the American River to the north.

Return the way you came.

24 WHITE PASS TO CHINOOK PASS THRU HIKE

Distance: 27 miles one way	
Hiking time: 3 to 4 days	
High point: 5,800 feet	
Elevation gain: 1,400 feet	
Season: Midsummer to late autumn	
Maps: Green Trails White Pass, No. 303; Bumping Lake, No. 271; and Mount Rainier East, No. 270	
Land manager: Naches Ranger District	

Hiking south to north, you'll find this section of the PCT is one of the easiest on the legs and on the eyes. The trail changes elevation gradually, if at all, throughout the hike, while the scenery of the William O. Douglas Wilderness Area provides a stunning foreground for sweeping views of the central Cascades. The trail crosses huge, green meadows, graced with

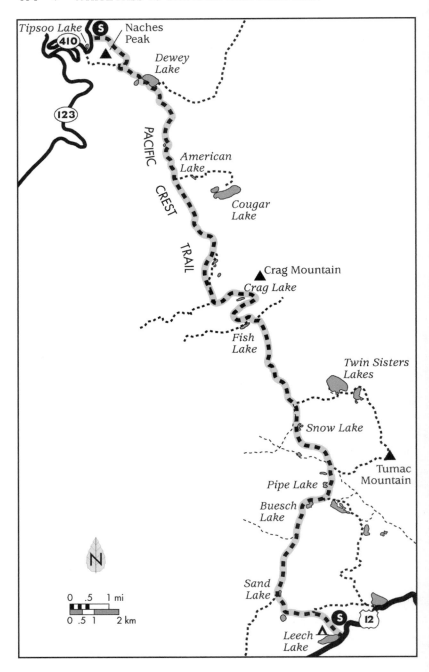

an array of wildflowers. Sparkling blue lakes litter the route like jewels dropped from the heavens. The summits of Mount Rainier, Mount Adams, the Goat Rocks Peaks, and the knobby tops of the lesser volcanoes of the William O. Douglas Wilderness Area—Mount Aix, Crag Mountain, Fryingpan Mountain, Bismark Peak, and Tumac Mountain—are all seen from various points on the journey.

To get to the southern trailhead, drive US 12 to White Pass. The PCT North Trailhead is found just east of the Ski Area at White Pass Campground. Turn onto a poorly marked road on the east end of Leech Lake and drive a few hundred yards to the trailhead, which is situated between the horse camp and the car campground. To reach the northern trailhead, drive east from Enumclaw on SR 410 to the summit of Chinook Pass. Park on the north side of the highway, either in the Lake Tipsoo Parking Area or just east of Tipsoo in a smaller parking lot, also on the north side of the highway. Cross to the south side of the highway to find the start of the trail.

From the southern trailhead, you'll start in the trees, climbing gradually to Sand Lake where you'll find the forest opens into a patchwork of meadows, woods, and lakes. The trail heads north to the trout-rich waters of Buesch Lake around the 6-mile mark. There are fine campsites at Buesch and for the next 5 miles as the trail weaves across a lake-studded basin between Tumac and Fryingpan Mountains. The first big lake you'll pass is Pipe, and the last in this stretch is Snow. In between are scores of unnamed ponds and potholes, many of which have excellent campsites nearby.

Just beyond Snow Lake, around the 12-mile mark, the PCT leaves the broad lake basin and heads north into the valley of Fish Creek. The trail descends along the creek to Fish Lake, 15 miles from the trailhead, before starting the steepest climb of the journey. The next 3 miles gain 1,500 feet as the trail climbs the flank of Crag Mountain, swinging east around Crag Lake, then back to the west to a ridge crossing at 5,700 feet.

From this point, the trail stays high, following the ridge crest north. The views will have been hit-or-miss so far, but from here on out, the views shine. Mount Rainier towers to the west, and the Goat Rocks and Mount Adams can frequently be seen to the south.

The remaining 10 miles of trail follow the boundary line between Mount Rainier National Park and the William O. Douglas Wilderness Area, veering west to enter the park, then back to the east to dip into the wilderness. All the while, Mount Rainier plays peek-a-boo on the western skyline.

The PCT near Carlton Pass, William O. Douglas Wilderness Area

In addition to the views, this stretch of trail has some of the most bountiful huckleberry meadows in the state. If the berries aren't ripe, don't fret, because the meadows will most likely be awash in colorful wildflower blooms. If the flowers are out, there's always a good chance of seeing wildlife in this remote area. Blacktail deer, black bear, elk, and armies of smaller critters (from coyotes to 'coons) thrive in this rich environment.

At Dewey Lake, about 24 miles from the south trailhead, the trail climbs moderately once more, gaining a little over 600 feet in a mile, to reach the wonderful meadows at the base of Naches Peak. Mount Rainier looms large now, towering just a few miles to the west of these meadows. The final 2 miles of the trek go too quickly as you enjoy the views of The Mountain all the way to the trail's end at Tipsoo Lake.

25 SOURDOUGH GAP

Distance: 7 miles round trip

Hiking time: 4 hours (day hike or backpack)

High point: 6,400 feet

Elevation gain: 1,000 feet

Season: Mid-July through October

Maps: Green Trails Mount Rainier East, No. 270, and Bumping Lake, No. 271

Land manager: Naches Ranger District

Seldom do you find a trail this gentle with such spectacular scenery. A pretty, clear-water lake, grassy wildflower meadows, and outstanding views await hikers willing to share the trail with lots of fellow nature-lovers and the occasional bear. (Where there are huckleberries, there are sure to be bears, and there are some wonderful huckleberry brambles above this trail.) Of course, with lots of meadows for grazing, rocks for hiding among, and trees to perch in, the area is also popular with a host of bird and animal species. Deer, mountain goats, hawks, falcons, marmots, martens, chipmunks, and the ever-faithful friend of hikers, gray jays, are just a few of the furred and feathered critters that thrive here.

With a modest elevation gain of just 400 feet in the first 2.5 miles, the trail can be enjoyed by hikers of all abilities—kids will love it, and

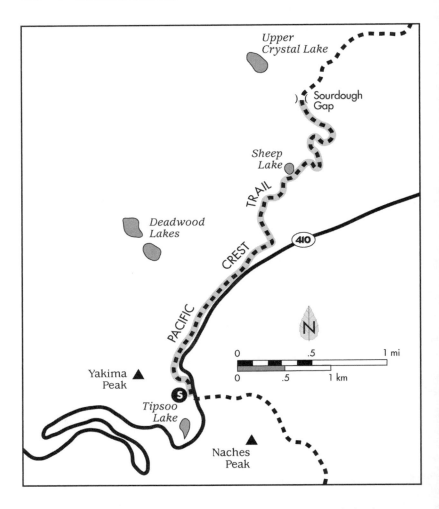

the idyllic little lake basin with its lakeside meadows and shady groves of trees, makes a great destination for the little tykes' first backpacking adventure.

To get there, drive east from Enumclaw on SR 410 to the summit of Chinook Pass. Just east of Tipsoo Lake, turn left (north) into a small trail-head parking lot on the north side of the highway. The trailhead is found on the backside of the lot, behind the restrooms. (Note: If the parking lot is full, return to the Lake Tipsoo Parking Area at the summit of the pass and hike the .25-mile trail around the lake to the lower lot and the PCT trailhead.)

The trail traverses the steep hillside meadows east of the pass, staying above SR 410 for the first mile. Traffic noise can be heard, and sometimes seen, through the brush and trees below the trail, but the views beyond make up for that. The deep valley of the Rainier Fork of American River, with Naches Peak rising on the far wall, is beautiful. If you have sharp eyes, or a good pair of binoculars, you can often pick out hikers rounding the flank of Naches on the PCT, some 3 trail miles to the south.

After the first mile, the trail veers north, climbing gently up to a bench below Sourdough Gap. Just past the 2.5-mile mark, you'll drop into the Sheep Lake Basin. There are nice campsites around the lake, but the best are on the small tree-lined knoll to the south of the lake. The trail to the Gap rounds the east side of the lake and begins a moderately steep climb up the valley wall to the rocky saddle of Sourdough Gap at 3.5 miles. Along the way, the trail loops through a few switchbacks and offers wonderful views down to the lake, and occasionally all the way back down to the trailhead.

Hikers resting on a knife-edge ridge above Sourdough Gap, looking over the valley of Crystal Lakes

Sourdough Gap is a small saddle in a jagged-edge ridge. You'll find a few spotty views of Mount Rainier during the approach to the gap, but for the really outstanding views, you'll need to scramble up the steep talus slope on the northwest side of the gap. A faint boot-beaten path leads to the ridge crest—be careful, though, because the far side of the ridge falls away as a 500-foot cliff. From this ridge, you'll be able to look southwest onto the Emmons Glacier of Mount Rainier. Directly below your vantage point is the Crystal Lakes Basin—be sure to wave to the hikers clustered on the shores of those pretty lakes.

If you would rather stick to the established trail, you'll have to forgo views of Mount Rainier, but by continuing on the PCT about .25 mile north of Sourdough Gap, you'll find wonderful views east into the meadows of upper Morse Creek, with the blue pool of Placer Lake sitting dead center in the valley. Far beyond is the long spine of American Ridge in the William O. Douglas Wilderness Area.

Return to the trailhead the way you came.

26 BULLION BASIN LOOP

Distance: 6.4-mile loop	
Hiking time: 4 hours	
High point: 6,300 feet	
Elevation gain: 1,600 feet	
Season: Mid-July through October	
Map: Green Trails Bumping Lake, No. 271	
Land manager: White River Ranger District	

Although this trail starts and ends in a developed ski area, the loop presents a natural wonderland of impressive proportions. The trail leads through steep, flower-filled alpine meadows, over narrow ridge spines, and under shady forest canopies. Views sweep over the dry, pine valleys of the eastern Cascades, the glacier-covered summit of massive Mount Rainier, and the craggy peaks of the central William O. Douglas Wilderness Area to the south. Best of all, despite the modest level of difficulty (not too long, not too steep), the trail isn't heavily used, so it's possible to find a quiet place for a peaceful lunch high on the ridge.

To get there, drive east from Enumclaw about 34 miles on SR 410

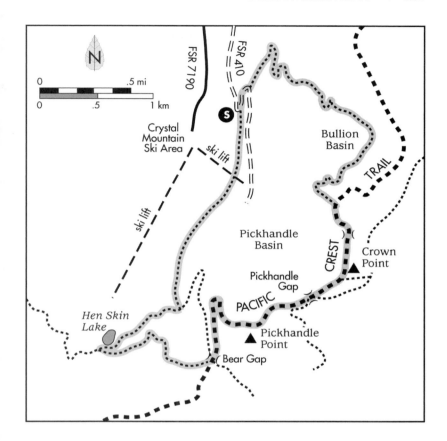

and turn left (east) onto Crystal Mountain Road (FSR 7190) leading to the Crystal Mountain Ski Area. Drive about 5 miles to the end of the road at the ski resort. Park on the left (east) side of the upper lot and find a faint trail behind the ski-school building.

The trail (Trail No. 1156) climbs northwest away from the main ski lodge toward some cabins on the east wall of the valley. In just a few hundred yards, you'll encounter a dirt access road. Continue up this road to the trailhead on the left.

For the first .5 mile the trail climbs gradually through open forests and meadows as it slants northeast before switching back to head up the Bullion Creek Valley into the heart of Bullion Basin. The basin, a flower-filled meadow in a shallow cirque, is reached in just under 2 miles. After crossing the creek, the path enters a deep thicket of woods and then jumps back into the sunshine as it climbs steeply for .5 mile to reach the junction with the PCT at 6,300 feet.

Turning south on the PCT, you'll follow the ridge down to Bluebell Pass, around Crown Point, and through Pickhandle Gap in the next 2 miles to reach Bear Gap (elevation 5,882 feet). These 2 miles are all well above treeline and offer constant views of the wildflower pastures at your feet and the panoramic vistas beyond. Though there are many sights to see every step of the way through this section, each pass and peak has its own special view: from Bluebell, look east to Fifes Peak; from Crown Point, look southwest to Mount Rainier; from Pickhandle, look southeast to American Ridge; and from Bear Gap, look north to Norse Peak, south to Mount Rainier, east to Fifes Peak, and west to Crystal Mountain.

Leave the PCT at Bear Gap by taking the right fork at the four-way

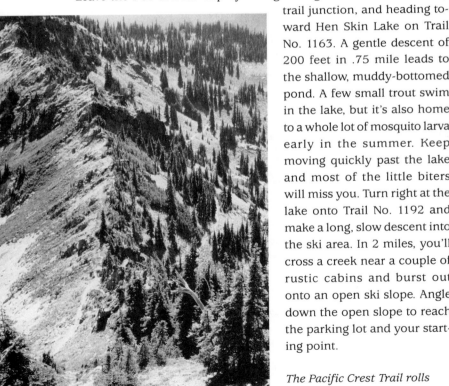

trail junction, and heading toward Hen Skin Lake on Trail No. 1163. A gentle descent of 200 feet in .75 mile leads to the shallow, muddy-bottomed pond. A few small trout swim in the lake, but it's also home to a whole lot of mosquito larva early in the summer. Keep moving quickly past the lake and most of the little biters will miss you. Turn right at the lake onto Trail No. 1192 and make a long, slow descent into the ski area. In 2 miles, you'll cross a creek near a couple of rustic cabins and burst out onto an open ski slope. Angle down the open slope to reach the parking lot and your starting point.

The Pacific Crest Trail rolls along a sharp-edged ridge near Bullion Basin.

271 NORSE PEAK LOOP

Distance: 11.5 miles round trip
Hiking time: 7 hours
High point: 6,858 feet
Elevation gain: 2,800 feet
Season: Mid-July through early October
Map: Green Trails Bumping Lake, No. 271
Land manager: White River Ranger District

Items to remember to bring on this hike: sunscreen, wildflower guide-book, sunscreen, plenty of water, sunscreen, camera, and sunscreen. You'll be on open, sun-drenched slopes nearly all the way up this steep trail, and it can get a bit warm. You'll need to bring plenty of water to stay hydrated, and—if you are like me—you'll be perspiring a lot, washing each application of sunscreen off in an hour or two. Fortunately, the stunning scenery along the route will keep you from moving too fast. The acres of wildflowers on all sides will capture your attention, and when

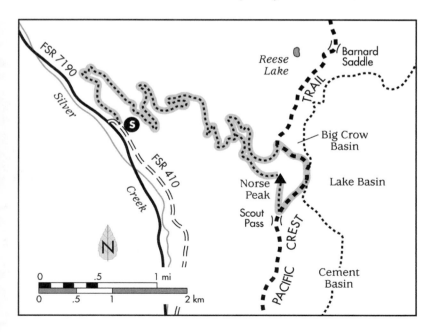

you tire of the rainbow of colors on the ground, you'll find new, breath-taking vistas around every corner.

To get there, drive east from Enumclaw about 34 miles on SR 410 and turn left (east) onto Crystal Mountain Road (FSR 7190) leading to the Crystal Mountain Ski Area. Drive about 3 miles to a large horse camp on the left (at a junction with FSR 7190-410). Park in the lot at the upper end of the horse camp and find the trailhead on the left (east) side of the parking area.

The trail (No. 1191) parallels FSR 7190-410 for more than .5 mile before turning uphill for a steep, hot climb through open, rocky mead-ows. In the first mile, the views are few, but as you pause periodically for a rest, glance south to see Mount Rainier rising over the ridge of Crystal Mountain. Each switchback in the trail brings more of the mighty moun-tain in view. By the time you reach the first trail junction (elevation 6,300 feet) 4 miles from the trailhead, the entire peak towers over the ski area and its namesake mountain.

Go right at this junction on Trail No. 1191A to continue your sweaty climb toward the summit of Norse Peak. In just 1.3 miles, you'll be stand-ing atop the 6,858-foot peak with 360-degree views. Because the former

A jagged ridge near Norse Peak

lookout site towers over the surrounding ridges and peaks, your views extend east past the Norse Peak Wilderness Area to Fifes Peak and Gold Hill. To the west, you'll see the sprawling patchwork forests of the central Cascades. This is checkerboard country—one square mile is U.S. Forest Service land, the next is private timber-company land. The squares, unfortunately, are easily discernible because most of the private holdings have been scraped bare by clearcutting. Fortunately, that is just one small part of the view.

Continuing south from the summit, descend a steep .5 mile (losing 600 feet) to a junction with the PCT at Scout Pass. Turn north on the PCT to start back around the flank of Norse Peak, and in .5 mile traverse the upper meadows of Big Crow Basin—a deep, natural wildflower bowl at the head of Crow Creek. Another .5 mile leads to a junction with Trail No. 1191—turn left onto this trail to complete your loop of Norse Peak and to return through the steep wildflower meadows to your awaiting vehicle. Going down, you'll find Mount Rainier slowly disappearing behind Crystal Mountain, like the setting sun slipping below the horizon.

28 HAYDEN PASS

Distance: 14 miles round trip	
Hiking time: 9 hours (day hike or backpack)	
High point: 6,300 feet	
Elevation gain: 2,300 feet	
Season: Mid-July through early October	
Map: Green Trails Bumping Lake, No. 271	
Land manager: White River Ranger District	

On a trail that offers outstanding views of Mount Rainier, you'd think that the big volcano would be the primary scenic draw. Rainier certainly does make a hike to Hayden Pass more enjoyable, but it's the features nearer at hand, together with the lesser peaks on the horizon, that make this hike special.

The ragged ridge of Castle Mountain—with its resident population of nimble mountain goats—the sparkling waters of Goat and Reese Lakes, and the thousands of acres of wildflowers are the features that draw me back to this section of the PCT.

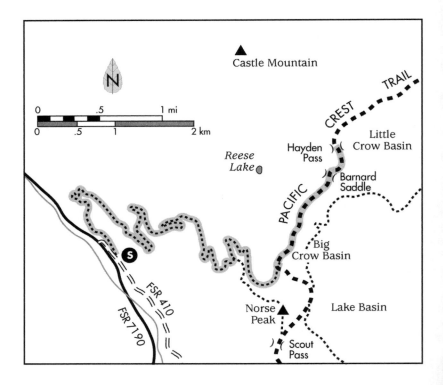

To get there, drive east from Enumclaw about 34 miles on SR 410 and turn left (east) onto Crystal Mountain Road (FSR 7190) leading to the Crystal Mountain Ski Area. Drive about 3 miles to a large horse camp on the left (at a junction with FSR 7190-410). Park in the lot at the upper end of the horse camp and find the trailhead on the left (east) side of the parking area.

Heading up Trail No. 1191 toward Norse Peak, you'll find you have to earn the rewards of the upper trail. The trail climbs steeply for 4 miles in open, sun-filled meadows. Come August, the hiking is hot, hard work, but as you ascend the meadows, the views gradually improve, with Mount Rainier slowly rising over Crystal Mountain to the southwest and the meadows growing more lush with colorful wildflowers.

At the 4-mile mark, the trail forks. The right fork leads to Norse Peak. Stay left on Trail No. 1191 and reach the PCT in another 1.2 miles at the ridge above Big Crow Basin. Turning north on the PCT, you'll find yourself forgetting about the wonderful views of Mount Rainier at your back and instead focusing on the awesome sight of the ridge-riding trail spread out before you.

As you follow the ridge crest between Big Crow Basin on the right and Goat Creek Valley on the left, keep an eye on the craggy peaks of Castle Mountain (really, a mile-long ridge of rock), and you might see some of those small patches of snow on its side jump from one rock to another. Wait a minute! That's not a patch of snow, it's a mountain goat—and there's another! And another! Castle Mountain is classic goat habitat—high, rocky cliffs, with a lot of steep meadow country around the base of the cliffs—and the goats know it. They love this mountain, and they often show off their high-elevation antics for PCT hikers.

The trail maintains a good view of Castle Mountain as it continues north, passing Barnard Saddle about 6.5 miles from the trailhead before dropping to Hayden Pass on the ridge between Little Crow Basin on the right and Reese Lake/Goat Lake Basin on the left. Faint, boot-beaten side trails lead down into both basins, but if you are backpacking, you'll find the best campsites in the flower-filled meadows of Little Crow Basin.

If you have extra energy on the return trip, you can add a few more miles to your trip distance by swinging out to do a reverse Norse Peak Loop (Hike 27).

The ridge-top near Hayden Pass offers excellent 360-degree views.

29 ECHO LAKE LOOP

Distance: 20-mile loop

Hiking time: 2 days

High point: 5,900 feet

Elevation gain: 2,400 feet

Season: Mid-June through early October

Map: Green Trails Lester, No. 239

Land manager: White River Ranger District

Want solitude on the PCT? This could be your best chance to find it while also finding a remarkably scenic forest in the heart of the Norse Peak Wilderness Area. The trail sticks to a deeply forested ridge, passes a few craggy rock outposts with fabulous views, and dips into a cool river valley where it passes a wonderfully clear, cool lake with many fine campsites and good fishing opportunities.

The trail begins humbly, with the trailhead perched on the upper edge of a clearcut and a first .5 mile of trail that cuts through a thin, second-growth forest still marred by slash piles of rotting trees. But while much of the Greenwater River Valley has been razed by logging companies, this long loop rambles through some of the last remnants of ancient Douglas-fir forests that blanketed the entire central Cascades not too many years ago.

As you explore this wild, scenic loop, give a moment's thought to the perils facing the PCT. This loop starts just south of Government Meadows, the old wagon road that runs through Naches Pass (now used extensively by four-wheel-drive fanatics). The PCT south of Naches Pass stays in the protective folds of the Norse Peak Wilderness Area, but just north of Government Meadows, it enters a world of checkerboard land ownership where every other square mile of forest has been leveled by chainsaws and bulldozers. From Naches Pass to Snoqualmie Pass, the PCT is a trail in trouble—that section is so mistreated that it is occasionally forced out of the clearcuts and onto logging roads.

The key is to keep your eyes facing south from the Meadows, and enjoy the wonders of the Echo Lake Loop, then when you get back home, contact your representatives in Congress and let them know what you think of having a national treasure like the PCT obliterated by clearcuts.

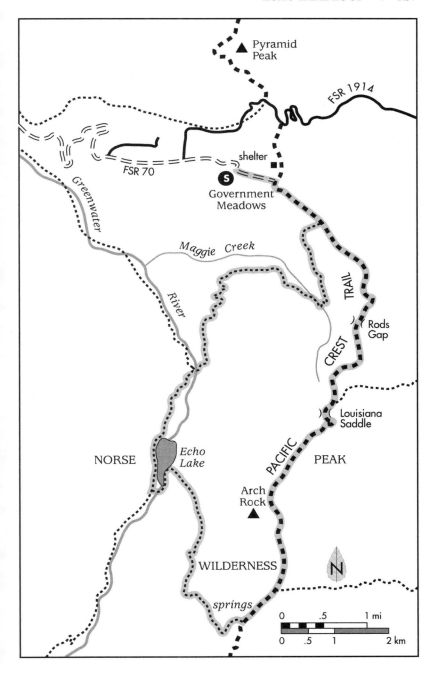

Pyramid
Peak

FSR 1914

shelter

FSR 70

S

Government
Meadows

Greenwater

Maggie Creek

River

TRAIL

Rods
Gap

CREST

Louisiana
Saddle

NORSE

Echo
Lake

PACIFIC

PEAK

Arch
Rock

WILDERNESS

N

springs

| 0 | .5 | 1 mi |
| 0 | .5 | 1 | 2 km |

To get there, from Enumclaw, drive east on SR 410 to the small town of Greenwater. About 1 mile east of the Greenwater Fire Station (on the east end of the community), turn left (north) onto the Greenwater River Road (FSR 70). Drive about 15 miles to the Naches Pass Trailhead at the road's end in an old clearcut. Note that the last mile of road is dusty, rough, and at times, deeply rutted. Use care when traveling it, especially in passenger cars and other low-clearance vehicles.

The trail leaves the clear-cut at the trailhead on an old logging road that leads into the trees. In a half-mile, the broad connector trail ends at a junction with the PCT. Turning left leads you to Government Meadows in about .5 mile. These broad, marshy meadows are a haven for deer and elk, and they are worth a visit if you have the time and inclination to go look for critters. The loop route, though, begins by turning right (south) on the PCT. The trail is fairly flat for the next few miles as it weaves through the thick, old forests. About 1 mile from the trailhead, a secondary trail leads off to the right. This is the other end of your loop route—stay left on the PCT, knowing you'll be returning via that side trail.

In about 3 miles, you'll find your first chance at a view. Just before the trail starts to descend into a few switchbacks down to Rod's Gap, you'll find a small clearing on the left side of the trail. Looking south and east, enjoy the view of rolling hills and gray-green forests spread out before you, but beware of the disappointment of looking northeast where you'll see huge scars on the land beyond the wilderness boundary.

Rod's Gap is a small, forested saddle on the ridge separating the

The cabin/shelter at Government Meadows

Greenwater River Valley from the Naches River Valley. From the gap, the trail turns upward and climbs during the next 5 miles. Just a mile past Rod's Gap, you'll cross Louisiana Saddle near a junction with a trail (Trail No. 945) on the left. Continue upward on the PCT, and you'll encounter a few clearings along the ridge where views of the nearby peaks present themselves. To the southeast, you'll see the rocky top of Raven; directly ahead is the prominent peak of Arch Rock.

The trail passes Arch Rock about 7 miles from the trailhead, and for the next mile, the trail stays on the open slope on the flank of the peak before reentering forests near another trail junction (Trail No. 951) on the left. Stay to the right on the PCT, and in .7 mile, at 5,900-feet elevation, veer right on the Echo Lake Trail (No. 1187). You can find campsites in the next .5 mile as the trail crosses a couple of small, spring-fed creeks before dropping 2,000 feet in 3 miles to reach the shores of Echo Lake.

This pretty forest lake offers excellent camping along its southern and eastern shores—the west shore is closed to camping—with many sites offering great views of the spires of Castle and Mutton Mountains to the southwest.

The Echo Lake Trail ends at a junction with the Greenwater Trail (No. 1176) on the south shore of the lake. Turn right (north) onto this trail, and drop down the Greenwater River Valley for nearly 2 miles before turning right onto Trail No. 1186 and climbing back to the PCT at a gradual rate of 1,400 feet in 5 miles. Back on the PCT, turn north, and in .5 mile, bear left onto the connector trail back to the trailhead.

30 CHINOOK PASS TO SNOQUALMIE PASS THRU HIKE

Distance: 69 miles one way; 23 miles one way to Naches Pass

Hiking time: 6 to 7 days; 2 to 3 days to Naches Pass

High point: 6,440 feet

Elevation gain: Loss of 3,410 feet; loss of 1,640 feet to Naches Pass

Season: Mid-July through early October

Maps: Green Trails Mount Rainier East, No. 270; Bumping Lake, No. 271; Lester, No. 239; and Snoqualmie Pass, No. 207

Land manager: White River Ranger District

There's only one reason to thru-hike from Chinook Pass to Snoqualmie Pass—to be able to honestly say you've done it. However, if you are more

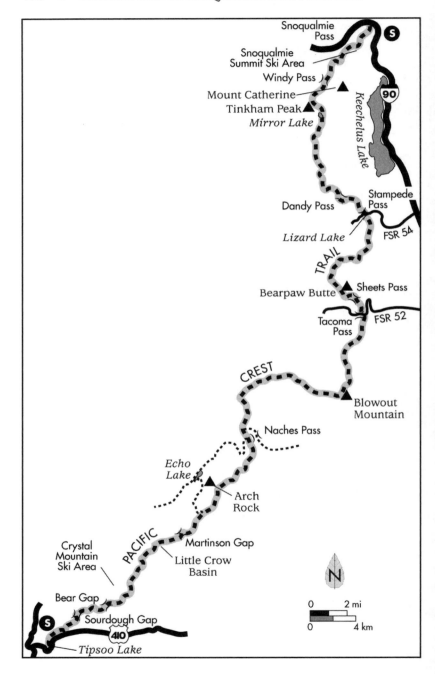

interested in natural beauty and scenic splendor than in covering every mile of the PCT, consider hiking the section from Chinook to Naches Pass and skip the clearcut-heavy trail north of Naches.

The lower half of this thru hike covers some beautiful terrain with awesome views of Mount Rainier and the mountains of the Norse Peak Wilderness Area. There are miles of ridge-top meadows to explore and deep, shady forests to enjoy. You'll pass a few alpine lakes and have a chance to see a variety of wildlife as you travel through some prime mountain-goat country and the home range of one of Washington's largest elk herds.

To get to the southern trailhead, drive east from Enumclaw on SR 410 to the summit of Chinook Pass. Just east of Tipsoo Lake, turn left (north) into a small trailhead parking lot on the north side of the highway. The trailhead is found on the backside of the lot, behind the restrooms. (Note: If the parking lot is full, return to the Lake Tipsoo Parking Area at the summit of the pass and hike the .25-mile trail around the lake to the lower lot and the PCT trailhead.) To reach the northern trailhead, drive I-90 to Snoqualmie Pass and take the Snoqualmie Pass West exit. Park near the USFS Visitor Center on the frontage road just east of the highway exit. To get to the Naches Pass Trailhead, see Hike 29.

Starting from Chinook Pass, the trail gradually ascends to Sheep Lake and Sourdough Gap in the first 3.5 miles. From the trailhead, you'll be hiking in subalpine meadows awash in wildflowers, and the views are wonderful from the first step on the trail. From Sourdough, the trail turns northeast and follows the high ridge above the Crystal Mountain Ski Area to Bear Gap. The next few miles stay on the knife-edge ridge between the ski area and the American River Valley. The panoramic views sweep in Mount Rainier and Mount Adams (on clear days) to the south, Gold Hill and Fifes Peak to the east, and Norse Peak to the north.

The high, rocky ridge-walk continues through Pickhandle Gap, Bluebell Pass, Scout Pass, and Barnard Saddle before skirting the east end of Castle Mountain near Little Crow Basin, 10 miles from the trailhead. Excellent campsites can be found in the meadows of Little Crow Basin and just below the trail to the west at Reese Lake on the flank of Castle Mountain. Watch the rocky cliffs of the Castle for the ever-present herds of mountain goats.

From Little Crow Basin, the trail continues north in meadows and thin stands of forest to Martinson Gap. In another 4 miles, the trail climbs over Arch Rock (5,920 feet) and passes a small spur trail leading to a

Sheep Lake, below Sourdough Gap, on the PCT north of Chinook Pass

rustic, old shelter on the flank of the Rock, about 18 miles from the trailhead. The trail descends rapidly into the trees now as it heads north through the heart of the Norse Peak Wilderness Area. Five miles from Arch Rock, a small connector trail on the left leads off to the Naches Pass Trail. This is the end of the trail if you want to avoid the clearcuts to the north.

If you want to head for Snoqualmie Pass, continue north past the rolling green expanse of Government Meadows and descend into the clearcuts around Pyramid Peak. The trail crosses a dirt road just past the meadows, and then follows a line of trees down to a clearcut at the base of Pyramid. The trail disappears, but signs lead up a narrow logging road through the clearcuts around the west side of the peak. The road fades into trail, and the trail turns east, paralleling FSR 7038 for the next 5 miles before crossing the road at Green Pass and then ascending to the summit of Blowout Mountain. From Blowout, 1 mile of trail passes through nice wildflower meadows on the ridge tops before the trail drops into the forest and heads due north to Tacoma Pass and Sheets Pass. In the 2 miles between these two passes, the PCT crosses a couple of logging roads, and views from the passes are limited to peeks of Mount Rainier beyond a growing sprawl of clearcuts.

North of Sheets Pass, the trail meanders up and down ridges, through dense second-growth forests and wide-open clearcuts, and over several dirt roads. At Stampede Pass, 50 miles north of the trailhead, the PCT crosses FSR 54 and passes Lizard Lake. The next 10 miles involve a number of road crossings and possible encounters with logging trucks and ATVs. At 60 miles, the trail passes Mirror Lake, and for a few miles it offers a pleasant hiking experience in thick old-growth forests. From Mirror Lake, it's a gradual descent around the flank of Mount Catherine and down the ski slopes to Snoqualmie Pass.

31 KENDALL KATWALK

Distance: 11 miles round trip

Hiking time: 7 hours (day hike or backpack)

High point: 5,400 feet

Elevation gain: 2,700 feet

Season: Mid-July through early October

Map: Green Trails Snoqualmie Pass, No. 207

Land manager: Cle Elum Ranger District

Cut into the side of a granite cliff, the Katwalk offers a remarkable hiking experience—the opportunity to stride on a narrow shelf hundreds of feet in the air. Actually, the Katwalk isn't really narrow. Rather than a typical trail tread of 20 or 24 inches, the Katwalk is a good 4 or 5 feet wide as it

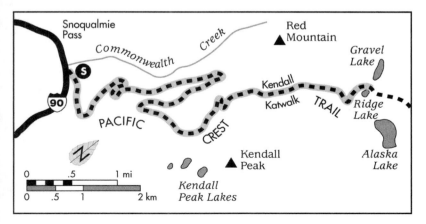

stretches across a vertical cliff face on the ridge between Kendall Peak and Red Mountain. The trail, blasted into the cliff face by dynamite crews hanging suspended from ropes, is perfectly safe once the winter's snow has completely melted off. However, if there is any lingering snow on the Katwalk, don't attempt to cross it—the Katwalk is not the place to slip and fall on a snow patch.

There is, of course, more to this hike than just the Katwalk. The PCT climbs from Snoqualmie Pass, cuts through old-growth forests, dances through a log-littered avalanche slope (a perfect place to see just how powerful an avalanche can be), and traverses broad, steep-sloped wild-flower meadows. Just beyond the Katwalk, you will find great campsites at a pair of small alpine lakes.

To get there, drive I-90 to Exit 52, signed Snoqualmie Pass West. At the bottom of the exit ramp, turn left (north), cross under the freeway, and in about 100 yards, turn right onto a dirt road leading into the PCT trailhead parking area.

The trail climbs into the trees above the parking lot and makes a long, lazy sweep east before rounding a hairpin turn to return west across the lower end of an avalanche slope. The jumble of trees piled around the trail illustrates how powerful a little snow can be when it starts to

The PCT with a view of Red Mountain near Kendall Peak

slide down a hill. The trail stays in the trees for the first few miles, passing a side trail to Commonwealth Basin at 2.5 miles.

Just past that junction, the trail steepens into a series of long switchbacks. The forest thins as the trail gains elevation, and about 3.5 miles into the hike, the forest starts to break up as small clearings and meadows appear. Soon the trail angles across the open meadows below Kendall Ridge. Red Mountain fills the skyline ahead while wildflowers color the ground around your feet.

These wildflower fields—known to some as Kendall Gardens—continue as the trail crests the ridge and angles north through a jumble of boulders on the ridge top. Finally, at 5.5 miles, the gardens narrow to a mere path, and the path suddenly disappears onto a broad shelf on the east face of the ridge. This is the Katwalk. If you are intimidated, turn back on the near side; or cross the Katwalk before you head back to Kendall Gardens for a leisurely lunch and the return hike to the trailhead.

If you want to spend the night, continue another 2 miles on relatively level trail to a pair of lakes that border the trail just below Alaska Mountain. The best campsites are found just south of Ridge Lake, but Gravel Lake (on the north side of the trail) also has a few good camp locations.

32 PETE LAKE LOOP

Distance: 22.5-mile loop

Hiking time: 2 to 3 days

High point: 5,500 feet

Elevation gain: 2,700 feet

Season: Mid-July through early autumn

Maps: Green Trails Snoqualmie Pass, No. 207; Kachess Lake, No. 208; and Stevens Pass, No. 176

Land manager: Cle Elum Ranger District

A modest hike up a spectacular river valley, a pretty little alpine lake, and a strenuous trek up and over a high, meadow-lined mountain ridge await you on this loop trip. If you are a more adventurous hiker, you can modify the route by adding excursions up to more remote and scenic lakes, down into deep river valleys, and/or around high, craggy peaks.

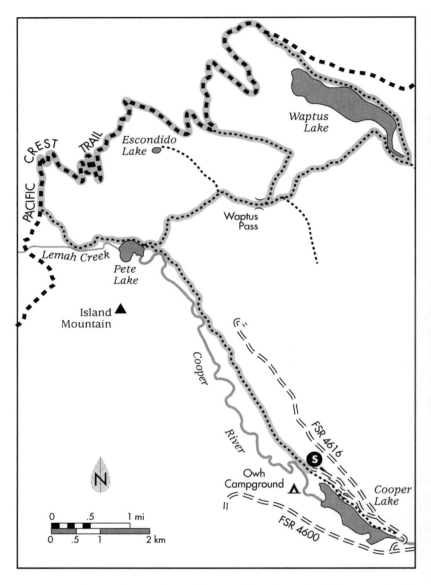

To get there, take Exit 80 off I-90 (signed "Roslyn/Salmon LaSac") and head north on the Salmon LaSac Road about 15 miles, passing through Roslyn and past Cle Elum Lake. Turn left (west) onto FSR 46 and drive 5 miles to Cooper Lake. Turn right onto FSR 4616, crossing Cooper River, and continue 1 mile past the upper loops of the campground to the trailhead at the end of the road near the upper end of the lake.

The trail, No. 1323, follows the broad Cooper River Valley upstream for 4.4 miles to Pete Lake. The valley is blanketed with thick, old-growth forest and the occasional river meadow, but few views. Pete Lake, though, offers good views of Summit Chief Mountain to the west and the surrounding ridges. The lake boasts good campsites, but because it is easily reached, the camps tend to fill up fast on hot summer weekends, and the rustic shelter near the lake seems to always have someone lingering in it.

The trail skirts along the eastern and northern sides of the lake before heading up the Lemah Creek Valley. The trail climbs steeply along the creek to a junction at 6 miles. Stay right on Trail 1323.2, which heads .75 mile up to Lemah Meadows on the PCT. (The left fork slants south toward Spectacle Lake.) Camp possibilities can be found in the meadows along the PCT; good water is available from Lemah Creek, which crosses the trail just south of where you join the PCT. From the meadows, you'll find wonderful views of Summit Chief Mountain.

Once on the PCT, head north as it continues up the north fork of Lemah Creek. After less than 1 mile of walking on the PCT, the trail turns steep as it climbs a long series of switchbacks in the next 5 miles. Along the way, you'll find increasingly fine views as the forest gives way to broad, open meadows. In addition to Summit Chief Mountain, you can look north to the glacier-covered summit of Mount Daniel. As the trail crests the 5,500-foot level on the ridge above Escondido Lake, the route levels out and traverses the meadows past a few small tarns—and a couple of nice campsites—before starting a slow descent toward Waptus Lake, which is seen to the north in the valley far below.

Avalanche lilies brighten the trail to Pete Lake.

Before dropping too far, though, you'll leave the PCT. At the 5,200-foot level—about 13 miles from the trailhead—look for a junction with a small trail leading off to the right. While the PCT continues north, Trail No. 1329.3 descends southeast to Waptus Pass, at the 16-mile mark. Note: You can add about 8 miles to your total loop distance by continuing to Waptus Lake, circling around its northern shore, and then climbing to Waptus Pass on Trail No. 1329.

From Waptus Pass, turn right onto Trail No. 1329 and descend through a steep series of switchbacks to the shores of Pete Lake. A quick left turn onto Trail No. 1323 returns you to your starting point.

33 CATHEDRAL ROCK–DECEPTION PASS LOOP

Distance: 14 + -mile loop

Hiking time: 2 to 3 days

High point: 5,500 feet

Elevation gain: 2,300 feet

Season: Mid-July through early October

Map: Green Trails Stevens Pass, No. 176

Land manager: Cle Elum Ranger District

Wow!

That was my first impression after exploring this loop and its many side-trip options. The fact that the drive to the trailhead leads up through one of the most beautiful mountain valleys you'll ever encounter is an indication of just how wonderful this trail is. The route offers a taste of some of the finest meadows, deepest lakes, and craggiest mountains in the Alpine Lakes Wilderness Area, all in an easy loop hike.

To get there, take Exit 80 off I-90 (signed "Roslyn/Salmon LaSac") and head north on the Salmon LaSac Road (FSR 4330) about 15 miles, passing through Roslyn and past Cle Elum Lake. At Salmon LaSac Campground, the paved road ends. Stay right on the main road (rather than entering the campground) and continue up the Cle Elum River Valley for another 12 scenic miles through beautiful meadows to the end of the road. Just before entering the Tucquala Meadows Campground, turn left into a wide trailhead parking lot.

From the parking area, hike down a short dirt road to the Cle Elum

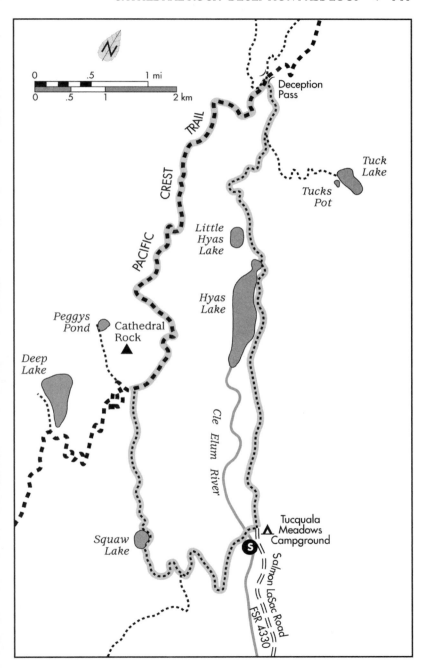

River and find the trailhead at a bridge over the river. Head up Trail No. 1345, climbing modestly in the first 2 miles (gaining 1,000 feet) to a junction with Trail 1322. Stay right to continue on Trail 1345 as it turns north along a long ridge crest. The forest on the ridge is broken and offers frequent views out across the Cle Elum River Valley to the Wenatchee Mountain Range on the opposite valley wall.

At 2.5 miles, the trail passes Squaw Lake. This is a popular camping destination for novice backpackers or families with small children—the hiking distance isn't too great, and the shallow lake is perfect for wading or swimming.

As you continue past Squaw Lake, the trail follows the ridge north, alternating through meadows and forest with a few small tarns dotting the meadows along the way. At 4.5 miles, the trail ends at a junction with the PCT. At this point, you're directly under the towering spire of Cathedral Rock. Look closely and you might see some Spiderman-wannabes scaling the rocky walls of the peak—Cathedral is quite popular with rock climbers.

Once at the PCT, you have a choice to make. To keep the loop short, head north to Deception Pass. If you've got time to spare, turn south and descend 3.5 miles to Deep Lake—a wonderful backpacking destination. In midsummer the broad meadow is awash with the purples and reds of thousands of blooming lupine and paintbrush. On the north end of the lake, the glaciers and snowfields of Mount Daniel feed a score of thundering waterfalls that grace the steep wall above the lake. The best camps are on the west side of the lake. Return north to Cathedral Rock to complete the loop.

From the junction at Cathedral Rock, head north around cliffs at the base of the spire, and in 2 miles, cross the first of two streams. In midsummer, the streams can usually be forded easily. But early on, when the snowmelt is feeding the creeks, the water can be high and dangerous, effectively closing the trail. Call the ranger station before you leave for your hike to check the river conditions.

The trail traverses out around the slope at the base of Mount Daniel and cuts through a series of broad meadows with fabulous views of the big peak and the rocky ridge of Granite Mountain and the Wenatchee Mountains across the valley. At 9 miles from the trailhead (not counting the side trip to Deep Lake), the trail crosses Deception Pass in a sun-filled old-growth forest. Leave the PCT here and turn right onto Trail No. 1376 to descend into the upper Cle Elum River Valley. A 5-mile hike down the valley, passing Hyas Lake along the way, leads you back to the trailhead.

Campers bivouac near Cathedral Rock along the PCT.

In addition to the Deep Lake side trip, you can split off the loop route at Deception Pass and climb Trail No. 1066 for 4 miles to Marmot Lake. Another option is to leave the trail just .5 mile south of the PCT junction at Deception Pass. A steep 2-mile climb on a faint trail (No. 1376.1) to the east leads to Tuck Lake, and another 1.5 miles of scrambling and hiking above Tuck Lake leads to Robin Lakes. These two lakes are nestled in a granite basin lined with larch trees (hence their nickname, the Little Enchantments).

34 SURPRISE AND GLACIER LAKES

Distance: 11 miles round trip	
Hiking time: 7 hours (day hike or backpack)	
High point: 5,200 feet	
Elevation gain: 3,000 feet	
Season: Mid-July through early October	
Map: Green Trails Stevens Pass, No. 176	
Land manager: Skykomish Ranger District	

Two cool, clear lakes at the base of a pair of jagged peaks await you on this route. Of course, the trail also includes the requisite wildflower meadows, stunning views, and scurrying wildlife—primarily pesky camp-robber jays and whistling marmots. The route to Surprise Lake has been discovered by the masses, but the pretty lake is worth sharing. If you are a solitude-seeker, you can always push on to the next lake along the trail or scramble up into the rocky meadows above the pools to find a quiet nook.

To get there, from Skykomish drive east on US 2 about 10 miles to the town of Scenic and turn right (south) onto a dirt road found just before the highway dips under a railroad trestle. At the next opportunity, turn right onto another dusty dirt road and follow it to its end. The trailhead is the wide spot at the road end, marked with a generic trail sign (i.e., a hiker silhouette).

The trail climbs away from the dusty trailhead and enters a clean, cool forest of ancient Douglas firs, hemlocks, and cedars. The trail parallels Surprise Creek for the next 4 miles to the lake, staying within the shady cover of the forest, always within hearing distance of the tumbling creek. From the sound of it, you'll know that water is crashing over a series of falls and through narrow rock chutes, and the frequent views

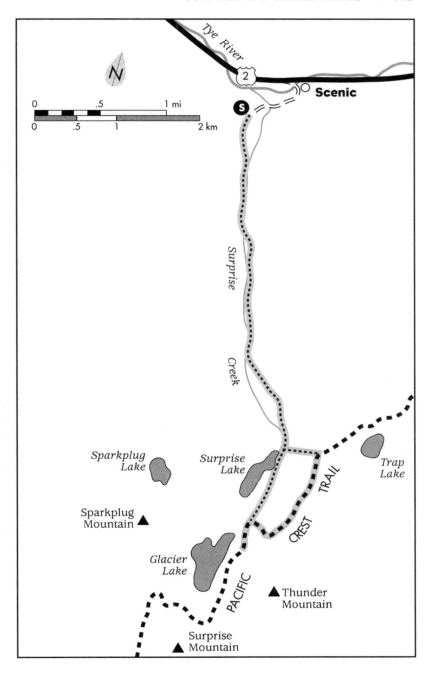

you'll have of the creek will prove that your hearing is dead-on. Countless waterfalls—some little more than whitewater rapids, others tumbling cascades—can be seen as you trudge up the trail.

The trail steepens in the last mile before the lake and crosses several sun-baked clearings, ensuring that you'll be hot and sweaty when you finally reach the shores of Surprise Lake. The rock-lined lake couldn't have been better designed for swimming—the rocky bottom keeps the water sparklingly clear, and the numerous rocks rising from the lake surface and lining the lakeshore make ideal sun beds. After a hot hike up a steep trail, there's nothing more refreshing than a plunge in a cold lake, especially when you can drag yourself out and recline on a flat rock that has been warmed by the morning sun.

Most day hikers (and a lot of backpackers) will stop at Surprise—and why not? In addition to the beauty of the lake itself, the lake basin offers stunning views of Surprise Mountain above. But to escape the crowds and explore the area a little further, head south on the trail for .7 mile to the PCT. Continuing south on the PCT for another .25 mile gets you to Glacier

Lake. Besides fewer people, Glacier Lake offers better views from its location nestled above treeline on the bench between Surprise Mountain, Thunder Mountain, and Sparkplug Mountain. Acres of heather meadows surround Glacier, and marmots continually whistle at the revelers around the lake.

When you've had your fill of lakeside views, leave Glacier Lake and head back north on the PCT, staying right when the Surprise Lake Trail veers off to the left. The PCT climbs the moderately steep slope at the base of Thunder Mountain, and then traverses north along its flank for 1.5 miles to the 5,200-

The trail to Surprise Lake

foot level. Here, a small side trail descends steeply to the left. Take this trail, dropping 700 feet in just over .5 mile to return to Surprise Lake. After another pause at the lake, head back down the trail along Surprise Creek.

35 JOSEPHINE LAKE

Distance: 9 miles round trip	
Hiking time: 7 hours (day hike or backpack)	
High point: 5,200 feet	
Elevation gain: 1,600 feet	
Season: Mid-July through early October	
Map: Green Trails Stevens Pass, No. 176	
Land manager: Skykomish Ranger District	

There's a strange dichotomy here—this trail begins by climbing the slopes of a developed ski area, but it soon leads to some of the most beautiful

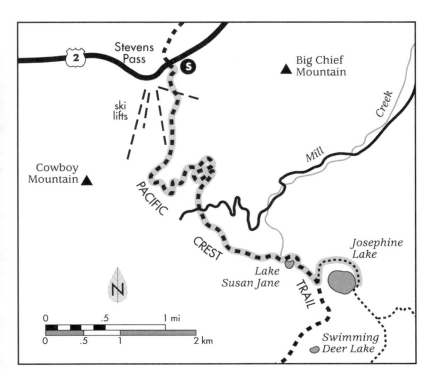

wilderness lakes you'll find anywhere. Dusty grassy-filled ski runs cover the first section of trail, musty old-growth forest towers around other parts of the lower trail, fragrant subalpine meadows grace high reaches of the route, and deep alpine lakes nestle alongside the path at multiple locations along the hike.

To get there, from Skykomish drive east on US 2 to Stevens Pass Summit and turn right (south) into a large parking lot just east of the ski area lodges and USFS cabins.

The PCT climbs south along the edge of the ski runs, proceeding up a series of switchbacks through the woods and open slopes between the lifts until it passes under one high ski-lift and crests a rocky ridge (5,100 feet) at the 1.5-mile mark. From here, the trail descends gradually through a talus slope, and in .25 mile, it cuts under a string of high-tension powerlines and crosses a narrow dirt service road alongside the wires.

After the service road, the PCT leaves the developed area behind and enters a world of pristine beauty. About 2.5 miles from the trailhead, the PCT enters the Alpine Lakes Wilderness Area as it contours along the face of a high ridge wall. The trail slices through fields of flowers with wondrous views east to Jill Hill Mountain and Nason Ridge.

The trail to Josephine Lake

Near the 3-mile mark, start a gentle descent of a few hundred feet to reach the shores of Lake Susan Jane at 3.5 miles (elevation, 4,600 feet). Nestled in a rocky cirque below the high, unnamed ridge, this tiny alpine lake is picture-perfect. Framed by cliffs and meadows, the lake offers views down the deep Mill Creek Valley and across to Big Chief Mountain. A few fine campsites ring the lake, but they get heavy pressure in midsummer. Better camps are found farther along the trail.

Leaving Lake Susan Jane, the PCT climbs back to the 5,000-foot level in the next .5 mile, cresting out in rock-lined meadows near a trail junction at the 4-mile mark. You have a hard choice here. You can continue south along the PCT to explore the sprawling high meadows and enjoy fantastic views of the Alpine Lakes Wilderness Peaks. Or you can turn left and descend the side trail (Icicle Creek Trail No. 1551) for .5 mile to Josephine Lake, with its splendid waterfront camps and views south into the Whitepine Valley and beyond to granite-faced Bulls Tooth Mountain.

Regardless of the choice, you won't be disappointed. Both options offer wildflowers, views, and a host of critters to keep you company. Don't believe me? Just hold a bit of gorp in the air and gray jays (a.k.a. camprobbers) will swoop in to welcome you. Or pause at the base of a rocky slope and listen to the whistles of marmots and the high-pitched "eeps" of pikas. Explore to your heart's content, and then return the way you came.

36 SNOQUALMIE PASS TO DECEPTION PASS THRU HIKE

Distance: 58 miles one way	
Hiking time: 5 to 6 days (minimum)	
High point: 5,930 feet	
Elevation gain: 2,900 feet	
Season: Mid-July through early autumn	
Maps: Green Trails Snoqualmie Pass, No. 207; Kachess Lake, No. 208; and Stevens Pass, No. 176	
Land manager: Cle Elum Ranger District	

The PCT bisects the heart of the Alpine Lakes Wilderness Area, exploring all it has to offer adventure-seeking hikers. Hike this long stretch of the PCT and you'll find deep old-growth forests, trout-filled rivers, and broad river-bottom meadows. Climb over high, rocky ridges and soak in panoramic views that sweep in a host of jagged peaks and up to five great

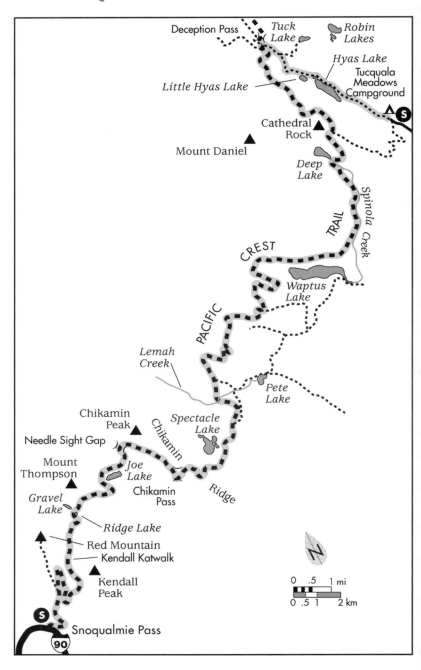

volcanoes—Mount Baker, Glacier Peak, Mount Rainier, Mount Adams, and Mount Hood can easily be seen from several points—and revel in the rainbow of wildflower bloom in the high subalpine meadows along the crest. And of course, there are lakes—from sprawling mile-long lakes in the valley bottoms to tiny alpine tarns surrounded by year-round snowfields. This is one of the most scenic and most accessible sections of Washington's PCT, and it is certainly worth setting aside a full week to explore it and all its side trails along the way.

To get to the southern trailhead, drive I-90 to Exit 52, signed Snoqualmie Pass West. At the bottom of the exit ramp, turn left (north) and cross under the freeway, and in about 100 yards, turn right onto a dirt road leading into the PCT trailhead parking area. To reach the northern terminus, take Exit 80 off I-90 (signed "Roslyn/Salmon LaSac") and head north on the Salmon LaSac Road (FSR 4330) about 15 miles, passing through Roslyn and past Cle Elum Lake. At Salmon LaSac Campground, the paved road ends. Stay right on the main road (rather than entering the campground) and continue up the Cle Elum River Valley for another 12 scenic miles to the end of the road. Just before entering the Tucquala Meadows Campground, turn left into a wide trailhead parking lot.

Beginning at Snoqualmie Pass, hike the steep 5 miles to Kendall Katwalk, enjoying the cool, old-growth forest and the ridge-top heather gardens. The Katwalk, cut into the solid granite cliff-face on the ridge below Kendall Peak, offers outstanding views—and it's the best place along the trail for you to determine whether you are afraid of heights. A couple miles farther on, you'll find the first, best campsites of the trip where the PCT traverses a short saddle between Gravel Lake and Ridge Lake.

The country around the PCT at this point is mostly open alpine meadows as the trail crosses the flank of Alaska Mountain. Four miles north of the two lakes, you'll reach the high point of this leg of the PCT—5,930-foot Needle Sight Gap on the south face of Chikamin Peak. At this point the trail turns south, traversing the rock gardens on the flank of Chikamin Ridge to Chikamin Pass at 5,700 feet.

Once through the pass, the PCT descends from the high rock meadows to lower alpine meadows around Spectacle Lake, and then continues north to Lemah Meadows. Here the trail really drops as it enters the valley of Waptus Lake—a long, deep lake nestled at 3,000-feet elevation below the glacier-covered peak of Mount Hinman. A 6-mile hike up the open, meadow-lined Spinola Creek Valley leads to the icy cold waters of

A small pond near Mount Daniel with views northeast across the Cle Elum River Valley

Deep Lake at the foot of Mount Daniel. Climbing the ridge east of Deep Lake, the PCT returns to the high country as it crests the ridge below Cathedral Rock at the 5,600-foot elevation. A long traverse north around Cathedral Rock and the flank of Mount Daniel—with two sometimes-tricky creek crossings along the way—leads to Deception Pass at the head of the forested Cle Elum River Valley.

Leaving the PCT at Deception Pass, descend 5 miles through the old-growth forests along Cle Elum River on Trail No. 1376 to the trailhead.

37 DECEPTION PASS TO STEVENS PASS THRU HIKE

Distance: 27 miles one way	
Hiking time: 3 to 4 days	
High point: 5,920 feet	
Elevation gain: 2,500 feet	
Season: Mid-July through early autumn	
Map: Green Trails Stevens Pass, No. 176	
Land manager: Cle Elum Ranger District	

This trail is a classic up-and-over move. A warm-up hike takes you up a cool river valley filled with a unique mix of towering ancient Douglas firs, cedars, and pines. A climbing traverse to the rocky ridges of the high country in the heart of the Alpine Lakes Wilderness Area, which is followed by a stroll across meadows and boulder fields—broken by the occasional pristine alpine lake—leads you to a steep drop to the trailhead at the far end of the route.

Along the way, the trail passes through prime blacktail deer habitat, under some golden eagle nesting grounds, and over countless marmot and pika burrows. If you visit in late summer, you may see black bears feeding on the rich huckleberry patches near Deception Lake and hear mountain goats kicking stones loose while prancing over the pinnacles of Surprise and Thunder Mountains.

To get to the southern trailhead, take Exit 80 off I-90 (signed "Roslyn/ Salmon LaSac") and head north on the Salmon LaSac Road (FSR 4330) about 15 miles, passing through Roslyn and past Cle Elum Lake. At Salmon LaSac Campground, the paved road ends. Stay right on the main road (rather than entering the campground) and continue up the Cle Elum River Valley for another 12 scenic miles to the end of the road. Just before entering the Tucquala Meadows Campground, turn left into a wide trailhead parking lot. (For the northern end of the route, from Skykomish drive east on US 2 to Stevens Pass Summit and turn right (south) into a large parking lot just east of the ski area lodges and USFS cabins.)

Heading up the Cle Elum River Trail No. 1376, past Hyas Lake, you'll gain just 1,100 feet in the 5 miles to Deception Pass and the junction with the PCT. These first miles serve as a great warm-up exercise for the more strenuous work ahead. As your legs get warm, you can enjoy the wonderful old-growth forest along the way, as well as the sprawling meadows around the blue waters of Hyas Lake, which are encountered after only 2 miles on the path.

At Deception Pass, turn north on the PCT and begin a climbing traverse of the wall above Deception Creek. About 3 miles from the pass, the trail breaks into open meadows with good views ahead to Surprise Mountain. In another .5 mile, pass Deception Lakes at 5,100 feet and climb to Pieper Pass on the south flank of Surprise Mountain. The trail turns sharply east at the pass (5,920 feet) and descends 2 steep miles to Glacier Lake (5,000 feet). After rounding the east side of the lake, the trail cuts up the forested side of Thunder Mountain to meadows at the 5,200-foot level. Travel the open country northeast to Trap Lake and follow a long ridge northeast to Hope Lake at the head of Basin Creek. This ridge, sporting broad huckleberry meadows in open forests, is a good place to spot wildlife of all

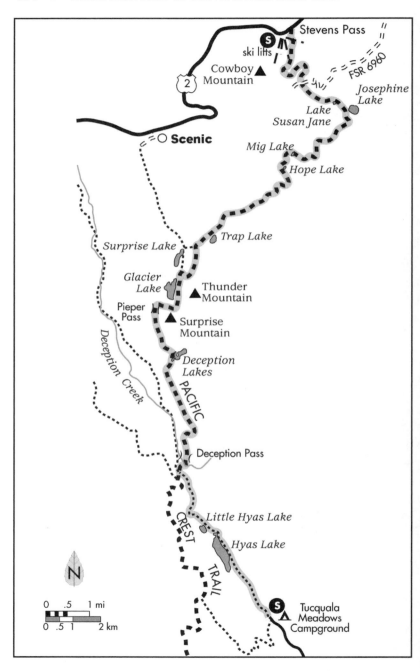

kinds and sizes, from berry-hungry black bears to berry-hungry chipmunks and berry-hungry grosbeaks.

An easy 3.5-mile climb past Mig Lake (limited camping at this small pond) to the rock-meadow ridge over Josephine Lake leads to the beginning of the end of the route. From Josephine, the trail drops to Lake Susan Jane, climbs a few hundred feet to an open ridge, and then descends into the Stevens Pass Ski Area. A fast walk down the trail alongside the ski runs brings you to the northern trailhead.

Hiker on a ridge-top boulder near Trap Lake

38 LAKE VALHALLA

Distance: 11 miles round trip
Hiking time: 7 hours (day hike or backpack)
High point: 5,100 feet
Elevation gain: 1,100 feet
Season: Mid-July through early autumn
Map: Green Trails Benchmark Mountain, No. 144
Land manager: Lake Wenatchee Ranger District

Today's hikers are fortunate. The great Norse warriors of old had to die a heroic death before ascending to Valhalla, the majestic halls of the Viking god Odin. The Vikings' Valhalla may have been a place of great beauty, but it surely could not have compared to the natural beauty of Lake Valhalla on the flanks of Lichtenberg Mountain.

Not only is the lake a thing of beauty—deep, clear, and sparklingly blue—but the deep, rocky cirque hanging above the Nason Creek Valley is magnificently scenic as well. Even the hike in to the lake is steeped in natural beauty. Long wildflower fields surround the trail, with views beyond to the peaks of the Henry M. Jackson Wilderness Area to the

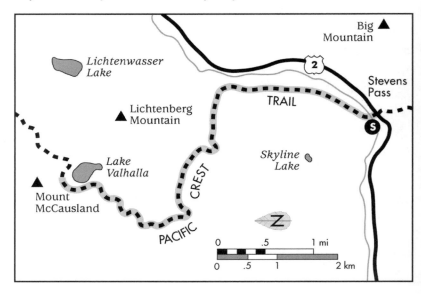

north and west and the Alpine Lakes Wilderness Area to the south.

To get there, from Skykomish drive east on US 2 to Stevens Pass. Continue to the east side of the pass and park in the large lot on the north side of the highway near an old, abandoned service station. The trailhead is found behind a large, blocky structure that serves as a power substation near the north edge of the parking lot.

The PCT crosses the highway at Stevens Pass and heads north along a long-abandoned railroad right-of-way, slanting east around the base of Skyline Ridge. The trail crosses steep, open hillsides above Highway 2, with excellent views east toward Jim Hill Peak and Nason Ridge.

At 1.5 miles into the hike, the trail climbs into the forest-lined Nason Creek Valley. A steep climb of the valley's headwall leads back into meadows around the 4,500-foot level, about 3.5 miles from the trailhead. Continuing to climb, the trail crosses a small ridge at 5,100 feet and drops the last .5 mile to the lakeshore (4,830 feet).

Lake Valhalla lies at the edge of a bench between Mount McCausland and Lichtenberg Mountain. There are some fine camps at the lake, and you can extend your adventures in any direction once you arrive. If

you're not tired yet, scramble to the 5,844-foot summit of Lichtenberg Mountain for outstanding views of the eastern slope of the Cascades, including stunning views of Nason Ridge and the Chiwaukum Mountains. If you're not feeling quite that energetic, continue north on the PCT toward Union Gap—just 2 miles north of Lake Valhalla. And if you're feeling truly lazy, head up into the meadows above the lake for a quiet siesta in the sunshine.

Return to the trailhead the way you came.

Hiker on the Lake Valhalla section of the PCT

39 LAKE JANUS–GRIZZLY PEAK

Distance: 6.5 miles (round trip) to Lake Janus, 16 miles (round trip) to Grizzly Peak

Hiking time: 5 hours to Lake Janus, 9 hours (day hike or backpack) to Grizzly Peak

High point: 4,700 feet (lake) / 5,600 feet (peak)

Elevation gain: 600 feet (lake) / 1,500 feet (peak)

Season: Mid-July through early autumn

Map: Green Trails Benchmark Mountain, No. 144

Land manager: Lake Wenatchee Ranger District

Long or short, the options of this route offer breath-taking beauty at every turn of the trail. If you're looking for a casual outing, you can stroll the forest path to the lake, enjoying views of the nearby peaks along the way. The lake is a sparklingly clear pond, with one half surrounded by forest and the other half bounded by broad heather meadows sporting colorful wildflowers early in the summer and crimson low-bush blueberry bushes later in the summer. (If you see hikers crawling around on their hands and knees, you can bet the 6-inch-tall plants have produced a fine crop of blueberries.)

For a longer outing, push on past the lake to the wonderful views from the summit of Grizzly Peak. This long trek can be done as a backpacking trip, but bear in mind that no reliable water source is available between Lake Janus and Grizzly Peak. If you don't want to pack water to a dry camp along the ridge, the best plan is to establish a camp at the lake and day hike to the peak from there.

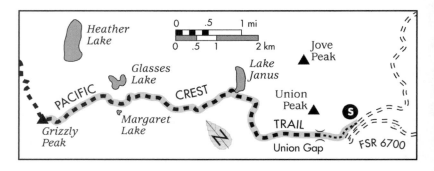

To get there, from Skykomish drive US 2 east toward Stevens Pass. Continue east another 4 miles past the ski area and turn left (north) onto FSR 6700 (Smith–Brook Road). Drive about 3 miles to a large switchback that turns to the right. The official trailhead is .25 mile up the road from the switchback, but it has limited parking. If the few spots in the pullout at the trailhead are full, return to the switchback and park in that broad pullout. Starting up the Smith–Brook Trail (No. 1590) through open forest, you'll climb the 500 feet to Union Gap in just under 1 mile. The trail ends at a junction with the PCT at Union Gap. Turn north and descend a steep, rocky slope below Union Peak into the head of the Rapid River Valley. The trail levels out along the valley headwall, sticking close to the fragrant fir forests for the next mile. As you near Lake Janus, the trail climbs gradually and the forests open slightly. The lake is about 3.2 miles from the trailhead and is ringed with trees and meadows. From the heather fields on the northwestern side of the lake, enjoy great views of 6,000-foot Jove Peak to the east. Camps can be found along the edge of the trees, set well back from the water's edge. (Although it's apparent that some folks have camped very near the lakeshore, these sites are officially closed in order to allow the vegetation to recover. In other words, for the good of the natural beauty and health of the lake basin, please resist the temptation to set up your camp near the water.)

From the lake, the PCT angles west through the woods as it climbs the far wall of the Rapid River Wall, topping out on a high ridge amidst meadows at 5,200 feet. If you don't mind the lack of water, you can find fine campsites at the edge of the meadows along the ridge crest.

With views of Scrabble Mountain to the west and Labyrinth Mountain to the east, the trail rolls north along the ridge crest. At 5.5 miles from the trailhead, you'll find yourself looking down on the blue jewel of Margaret Lake (on a bench below the left side of the trail), and shortly after, the much larger azure gems of Glasses Lake and Heather Lake to the right.

Just past the view of Heather Lake, the trail climbs, and at 8 miles out, it crosses the summit of Grizzly Peak—well, not quite. You'll have to scramble a few feet to the true top of the 5,596-foot peak. From the top, enjoy the 360-degree views of the surrounding wildernesses and marvel at the two worlds of the PCT. To the east, look down on the dry pine and spruce forests of the Little Wenatchee River and the dusty dry line of Wenatchee Ridge. Turn around and face west to see the emerald green forests of Douglas fir and hemlock in the Rapid River Valley.

Wildflowers and rocks near Grizzly Peak

The PCT continues north from Grizzly Peak, tempting you with another summit crossing in just .5 mile (an unnamed 5,500-foot peak). But remember that you have a long walk back to the trailhead, and the views from the next peak are much the same as the wonderful panoramic view from Grizzly, so you're better off simply enjoying a rest at the top of Grizzly Peak before heading home.

40 PEAR LAKE BASECAMP

Distance: 12 miles to basecamp
Hiking time: 2 days minimum
High point: 5,200 feet
Elevation gain: 1,400 feet
Season: Mid-July through early autumn
Map: Green Trails Benchmark Mountain, No. 144
Land manager: Lake Wenatchee Ranger District

All kinds of delicious views are sampled on this route—from the meadow-lined shore of Pear Lake to the scrumptious scenery at Peach Lake. Sure, you could day-hike to the lakes, but this area deserves a full tasting. To really savor the hike, plan a multi-day trip with a basecamp at the lake. After all, what could be better than making a modest hike to a pretty lake basin where you can pick a campsite alongside any one of a handful of gorgeous ponds, and then spend days exploring the world along the Cascade Crest?

To get there, from Lake Wenatchee drive west on the Little Wenatchee River Road (FSR 6500), and near the Riverside Campground, turn left

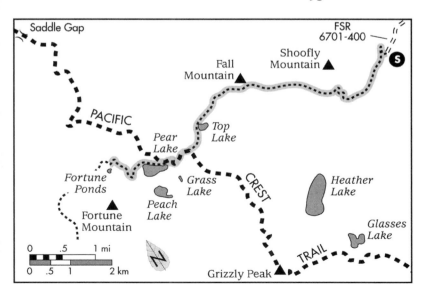

Peach Lake near the PCT

(south) onto FSR 6701, which follows the south back of the river upstream. In about 6 miles, turn left onto FSR 6701-400. (Note: The Green Trails map incorrectly shows this as FSR 500.) The trailhead is at the end of this road.

Starting up Trail No. 1506, you'll traverse a tree-covered slope on the flank of Shoofly Mountain, staying fairly level for 1 mile. The trail then steepens, climbing a long series of switchbacks and sloping north to the meadows under the summit of Fall Mountain. You'll cross a shallow saddle at 5,200 feet. Pause for a breather here, about 3 miles from the trailhead, and soak in the views of Shoofly and Fortune Mountains, with the Lake Creek Valley between.

From Fall Mountain, descend through meadows back into the trees, passing Top Lake before reaching Pear Lake at 6 miles (elevation 4,800 feet). Fine campsites are located near this meadow-lined lake. A short scamper through a small heather-filled saddle under Fortune Mountain leads to Peach Lake at the same elevation.

Once camp is established, enjoy exploring the region in the coming days. From Pear Lake, follow the PCT south through Wenatchee Pass and climb up onto the long, open ridge leading to Grizzly Peak. It's just 4 miles from the lake to the peak, but the views along the way are endless. The trail stays on the crest of the Cascades for those miles, offering stunning views east and west.

You might also consider heading north on the PCT. Again, the trail hugs the Cascade Crest, following meadows along the spine of the ridge, which separates the Cady River Valley from the West Cady River Valley. About 4.5 miles north of Pear Lake, the trail crosses Saddle Gap on the flanks of Benchmark Mountain. Another .5 mile of climbing gets you to a junction with the West Cady Ridge Trail. Head west on this route for 1 or 2 miles for outstanding views back toward the high summit of Fortune Mountain—your camp lies on the far side of the mountain. If you're a truly adventurous soul, you may want to scale Benchmark Mountain. Following the West Cady Ridge Trail east about 1.5 miles, you'll find a spur trail heading due north. This leads to the mountaintop (5,800 feet) in about .25 mile. If you thought the views were great from the ridge trail, you'll find your jaw dragging in the dirt at the top of Benchmark. To the north, Skykomish Peak, June Mountain, Long John Mountain, and Johnson Mountain stretch toward the clouds. To the east, Wenatchee Ridge—punctuated by the high peaks of Longfellow Mountain and Bryant Peak—cuts the horizon. To the south, Fortune Mountain stands like a sentinel marking your campsite.

Return the way you came.

41 SKYKOMISH PEAK CIRCUMNAVIGATION

Distance: 24 miles round trip

Hiking time: 3 days minimum

High point: 5,600 feet

Elevation gain: 3,100 feet

Season: Mid-July through early autumn

Maps: Green Trails Benchmark Mountain, No. 144, and Monte Cristo, No. 143

Land manager: Skykomish Ranger District

A word of caution: pack lots of film for this trip. A long, beautiful walk up a meadow-filled river valley leads to one of the prettiest alpine passes in the state. Click, click, click. The camera has seen lots of use already, right? No problem, but make sure you have enough film for what's ahead because the early section is just an appetizer for the main course. High, mountainous ridgelines; delicate alpine meadows; clear, cold lakes; and endless panoramic views come next. A long stroll down a rocky ridge—one side of which is forest, the other falling away in cliffs and rocky talus slopes—with more film-consuming views finally closes the loop.

To get there, drive US 2 to Index and turn north onto the North Fork Skykomish River Road (FSR 63) and continue to the trailhead at the end of the road, about 21 miles from US 2. Before starting the hike, note that the loop route ends at a trailhead 1.5 miles back down the road. If you'd prefer to walk the road at the beginning of your trek rather than at the end (I recommend getting the road walk out of the way early), draw straws with your hiking partners to see who gets to drive back down to the West Cady Ridge Trailhead and then walk the 1.5 miles back to the road end. The person with the short straw should leave his or her pack at the upper trailhead to make the road walk easier.

Heading up the North Fork Skykomish River Trail, enjoy the cool forests and periodic glades in the valley bottom. A junction with the Pass Creek Trail at 1.5 miles marks the end of an alternative (and shorter by 5 miles) loop if and when a bridge is ever built over the raging torrent that is the river here. Until that time, however, the Pass Creek Trail is not an option for hikers—the river crossing is too dangerous.

Continuing past the junction, you'll find the trail steepens and moves up the hillside above the river before dropping back to its banks. At the

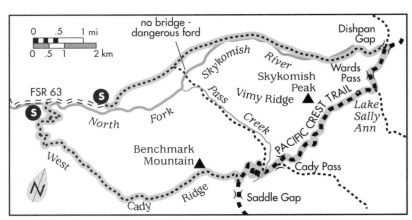

Binoculars are helpful for those who want to watch mountain goats on Skykomish Peak.

4-mile mark, the trail crosses the North Fork Skykomish River. No bridge exists at this crossing either, but the river is a bit slower and shallower than at Pass Creek, making a ford easier. Note: Early summer hikers may find the river too high to cross as the river swells with melting snow. Do not attempt the crossing if you are not sure you can do it, and never attempt a river fording alone. It is better to cut your hike short than risk injury or drowning during the crossing. You must know your limits, and then try never to exceed them.

Once across the river, the trail climbs a small ridge crest, cutting through a meadow—with good campsites—at 5 miles. Another 2.5 miles of steeper climbing gets you to the PCT at Dishpan Gap. Rock-studded meadows at the Gap provide wonderful views north to an unnamed peak directly above the Gap, and you'll want to snap a few pictures of Kodak Peak—even if you are using Fuji film!

Turning south on the PCT, leave Dishpan Gap and start a long, 5.5-mile hike through a continuous network of alpine meadows past Lake Sally Ann and around the east slope of Skykomish Peak. The trail crosses the rocky top of a 5,600-foot protuberance on the south side of Skykomish Peak and then descends to Cady Pass at 4,300 feet.

Just .5 mile south of Cady Pass, the Pass Creek Trail drops away to the right (west). It heads back down to the North Fork Trail in 3.5 miles, but again, it requires a tricky, sometimes dangerous, fording of the Skykomish River before returning to the main trail. Stick to the longer loop by continuing south on the PCT another 1.5 miles to the junction with the West Cady Ridge Trail (No. 1054).

Turn right off the PCT and head east on West Cady Ridge. For the next 6 miles, the trail rides the ridge crest with fabulous views south to Fortune Mountain, Fall Mountain, and the deep valleys of the Henry M. Jackson Wilderness Area. If you have the energy (and a few extra rolls of film), climb the spur trail found 1.5 miles east of the PCT. In .25 mile of steep climbing, you'll find yourself atop Benchmark Mountain. The views here are staggering. You can scan the entire Henry M. Jackson Wilderness Area from the long line of Wenatchee Ridge to the knobby top of Bald Eagle Mountain to the west. To the north, Mount Baker and Glacier Peak rise like white cones from the mountains around them, and to the south, Mount Rainier dominates the horizon.

The trail continues east through the meadows along West Cady Ridge to the very end of the ridge itself. The route then descends a steep 2 miles to the trailhead and, if you've planned ahead, your waiting car.

42 WHITE MOUNTAIN

Distance: 16 + miles round trip	
Hiking time: 2 days	
High point: 6,000 feet	
Elevation gain: 3,900 feet	
Season: Mid-July through early autumn	
Maps: Green Trails Glacier Peak, No. 112, and Sloan Peak, No. 111	
Land manager: Darrington Ranger District	

Between White Pass and Red Pass, the PCT slices through some of the most beautiful, and most fragile, alpine meadows found anywhere along its 2,600-mile length. Part of the beauty of the sprawling meadows is the backdrop. On the southern, White Pass, end of the meadows, the jagged top of White Mountain (7,043 feet) towers over mountain-goat pastures; from the northern end near Red Pass, the glacier-covered, rock-studded

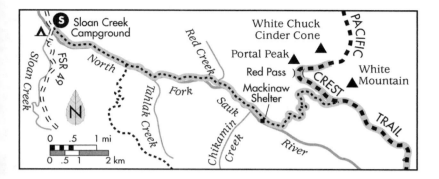

summit of Glacier Peak looms large over wildflower fields. The fact that you get to enjoy a long, scenic hike up the pretty Sauk River Valley to reach the alpine country only adds to the enjoyment you'll find on this outing.

To get there, from Darrington drive south on the Mountain Loop Highway 16 miles and turn left (east) onto the North Fork Sauk River Road (FSR 49). Continue about 7 miles east to the Sloan Creek Campground and trailhead.

Hiking east up the Sauk River Trail, you'll soon understand why the North Fork Sauk has been designated a National Scenic River—the tumbling, clear waters and pristine old-growth forest along its banks combine to create a level of natural beauty seldom found these days. The trail enters the Henry M. Jackson Wilderness Area in the first .5 mile.

The broad valley narrows rapidly, but the trail stays near the river, even as the walls close in around it. From the 2,100-foot trailhead, the trail gains little elevation until it reaches Mackinaw Shelter at 5.2 miles, at 3,000 feet. Many excellent campsites are located along the entire river valley, but the best may be here, near the old wooden shelter on the riverbank.

From Mackinaw, the trail continues about .5 mile upstream before turning vertical and making a long, slow climb through a seemingly endless series of switchbacks. How steep is it? In just under 3 miles, the trail gains 3,000 feet in elevation. Fortunately, the effort is worth it as the old-growth forests of the lower hillsides give way to vast alpine meadows near the junction with the PCT at 6,000 feet.

Here, some 8 miles from the trailhead, you'll be tempted to just plop down in the heather meadows and stare in awe at the surrounding views.

Juvenile marmots playing in meadows near White Pass

White Mountain looms overhead to the east, but its 7,043-foot summit is dwarfed by Glacier Peak towering over it at 10,541 feet. To the south, Johnson Mountain, Kodak Peak, and Skykomish Peak reach for the sky with Mount Rainier sometimes visible far off in the distance. To the west, Sloan Peak can be seen beyond the Sauk River Valley.

From the PCT junction, you can head back down, either to a camp at Mackinaw or all the way to the trailhead if you're energetic enough. If you're camping along the river, though, you can enjoy the high country around White Mountain as a day hike with a light pack, so you have the option of pushing on to further exploration. Turn south on the PCT to descend to White Pass and fabulous views toward the glacier-covered ridge of Indian Head Peak. Or head north on the PCT, and in 2 miles, cross Red Pass below Portal Peak. One mile past Red Pass, the trail skirts a small tarn at the base of the White Chuck Cinder Cone—a perfectly symmetrical volcanic cone rising from the rocky meadows on Glacier Peak's flank.

If you choose to make camp in the high country, the nearest water is just north of Red Pass at the small tarn, near the 5,400-foot level. Keep in mind the fragile nature of these high meadows and camp only in established sites to avoid damaging the slow-growing vegetation.

43 KENNEDY RIDGE

Distance: 18 miles round trip

Hiking time: 2 days

High point: 5,225 feet

Elevation gain: 3,000 feet

Season: Mid-July through early autumn

Maps: Green Trails Glacier Peak, No. 112, and Sloan Peak, No. 111

Land manager: Darrington Ranger District

The Cascade volcanoes are still very much alive, and if you've ever doubted it, just hike this route. The bubbling waters of Kennedy Hot Springs prove Glacier Peak is still astride a hot spring in the earth's crust. But while many casual hikers make the springs their destination on this trail, serious backpackers will skip the overused (and therefore bacteria-laden) springs and push on into the high country on the flanks of the big volcano. After all, you can soak in a hot bath at home, but how often do you get to experience the majesty of sleeping in a huge alpine meadow

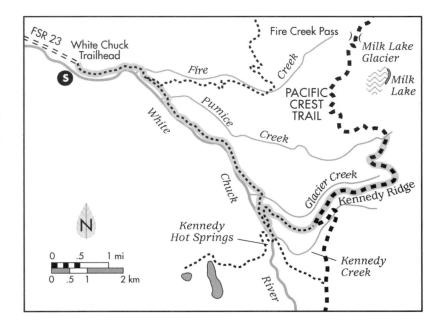

sprawled under the icy face of a glacier? Not often enough, no doubt, and the hike on Kennedy Ridge offers a multitude of high-country camps, each with uniquely beautiful views.

To get there, from Darrington drive 9 miles south on the Mountain Loop Highway and turn left onto White Chuck River Road (FSR 23) just past the Sauk River Bridge. Continue east on FSR 23 for 10 miles to find the trailhead at the road's end.

Head up the White Chuck Trail (No. 643), a wide, well-maintained path along the shores of the river. Deep, old forests surround the trail, keeping you cool even on the hottest summer days. In places, the valley narrows and the trail rolls under tall cliffs and across broken talus slopes. You'll have to contend with three stream crossings—over Fire, Pumice, and Glacier Creeks—but good footlogs or bridges are usually in place. The trail forks 5 miles from the trailhead. Continuing up the river, the main trail passes Kennedy Hot Springs in about .5 mile. The steaming water is refreshing in the middle of winter when you've struggled up the valley on snowshoes, but come summer, hundreds of people flock to the pool—which holds only four people at a time. On some weekends, campers queue up to take a dip in the natural hot springs. Unfortunately, all those bodies—some of which are not subjected to good personal hygiene—in a

There are plenty of streams to cross near Kennedy Hot Springs.

steamy pool of water creates a breeding ground for bacteria. If you must dip in the pool, wait until late autumn to visit, when the springs have flushed the worst of the bugs out.

Back on the trail, rather than continue up to the hot springs, take the left fork at the junction and climb Trail No. 639 up a steep 2 miles to a junction with the PCT at 4,200 feet. The trail is mostly in old-growth forest, but the occasional clearing provides views of Glacier Peak ahead and the White Chuck River Valley behind. Stay left on the PCT and continue climbing up the spine of Kennedy Ridge, leaving the forest behind and entering a world of volcanic rock and heather meadows. Of course, as the forest thins, the views improve. After 2 miles of hiking on the PCT, you'll reach a crossing of the headwater of Glacier Creek in a deep cirque at the base of Kennedy Peak and the Kennedy Glacier. Wonderful campsites are scattered throughout the meadows of this basin—although you should stick to previously established sites to avoid spreading the trampling of fragile meadow life.

If campers are already filling the basin, continue north on the PCT as it traverses 1 mile around the head of Glacier Ridge and leads into more meadow camps at the head of Pumice Creek. From either camp location, take some time to explore the world of rock and ice above you. Scramble up the slope to the base of the glaciers feeding the streams near camp. Kennedy Glacier feeds Glacier Creek; an unnamed glacier to the north feeds Pumice Creek.

Return the way you came.

44 MICA LAKE / FIRE CREEK PASS

Distance: 23 miles round trip	
Hiking time: 2 days	
High point: 5,443 feet	
Elevation gain: 3,000 feet	
Season: Mid-July through early autumn	
Map: Green Trails Glacier Peak, No. 112	
Land manager: Darrington Ranger District	

Hiking through an open forest of ancient trees, with Glacier Peak towering ahead, you'll wonder why anybody would choose to hike anywhere

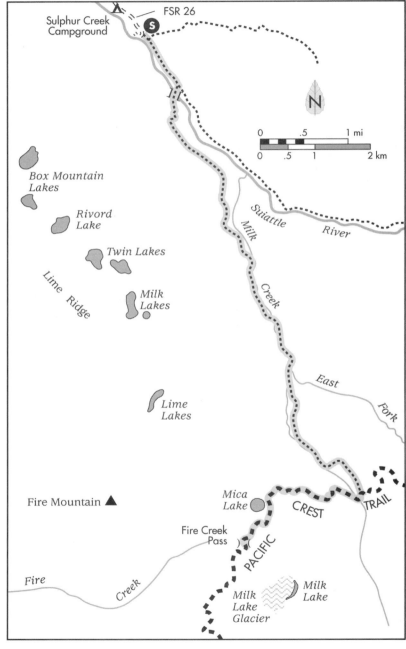

else but here. This is a scenic hike from start to finish, but it's the finish that will make you truly believe this is one of the most beautiful places on earth. The cool, blue pool of Mica Lake offers campers not only views of Glacier Peak but perfect reflections of its icy north face. Framing the reflected picture are fields of flowers—from pink heather to deep blue lupine. It's like camping in a painting in which the artist adds an endless array of beautiful elements. Not satisfied with just fragrant flowers and pretty mountains and lakes, the artist has also added mountain goats, golden eagles, and flocks of gray jays and other birds. Need more? Listen for the high-pitched whistle of marmots and the sharp "Eep!" of pikas scurrying among the rocks. This is a hike for all the senses.

To get there, from Darrington drive north about 6 miles on SR 530, and just after crossing the Sauk River Bridge, turn right (east) onto the Suiattle River Road (FSR 26). Continue 26 miles to the road end and trailhead.

The hike begins with 1 mile of walking on an abandoned section of dirt road. At the end of the road walk, two trails branch off. Stay right, cross the Suiattle River, and begin a gradual ascent of the valley wall on the south side of the river. As the trail traverses along the hillside, it passes through some of the most ancient groves of forest left in the Glacier Peak region. Look around and notice the massive western red cedars, Douglas firs, and hemlocks—some of these giants measure 10 to 15 feet in diameter and tower hundreds of feet into the air.

More than 3 miles into the hike, the trail descends slightly into a meadow in the bottom of the Milk Creek Valley. Here is the first peek of Glacier Peak, standing on the southern horizon at the far end of the valley. As the trail continues up Milk Creek, it crawls back into forest, coming out a time or two for views of the great volcano as you slowly climb upward toward its flanks.

Milk Creek is a pretty stream, and the broad valley bottom offers a multitude of campsites. But if you have the patience and strength to continue, push on. At 7.5 miles, the Milk Creek Trail ends at a 3,900-foot junction with the PCT. Turn south and trudge up a long, steep series of switchbacks ending at the shores of Mica Lake at 5,443-feet elevation, about 11.5 miles from the trailhead.

Mica Lake offers some wonderful campsites, set well back from the water, with eye-catching views south of Glacier Peak. Between the lake and the summit stands Kennedy Peak, and below that, a smaller peak

Blacktail deer at a small pond near Mica Lake

covered by Milk Lake Glacier, which seems to hang over the top of Mica Lake. To explore the area further, set up camp and then push on south another mile to Fire Creek Pass on the eastern shoulder of Fire Mountain. From here, look north down the Milk Creek Valley and along the jagged crest of Lime Ridge high above the valley.

Return to the trailhead by the same route.

45 SUIATTLE RIVER LOOP

Distance: 33-mile loop	
Hiking time: 3 to 4 days (minimum)	
High point: 6,000 feet	
Elevation gain: 4,400 feet	
Season: Mid-July through early autumn	
Maps: Green Trails Glacier Peak, No. 112	
Land manager: Darrington Ranger District	

A pair of gorgeous river valleys and a traverse of the north side of one of the most scenic mountains in the Northwest are all that await you here.

Well, that's not quite all. There are also thousand-acre meadows to explore, knobby peaks to see and scramble around, and wildlife to witness. Set deep within the Glacier Peak Wilderness Area, this loop covers wild, pristine country. It also provides a tiny taste of what PCT thru-hikers must endure daily on their 2,650-mile trek from Mexico to Canada—a seemingly endless series of climbs to high ridges and descents into deep valleys. Despite its name, the PCT doesn't stay atop ridge crests all the way from border to border, and this loop proves that point. The 15 miles of PCT covered on this loop hike begin near the ice fields of Glacier Peak and end alongside the waters of Suiattle River in a deep valley bottom.

To get there, from Darrington drive north about 6 miles on SR 530, and just after crossing the Sauk River Bridge, turn right (east) onto the Suiattle River Road (FSR 26). Continue 26 miles to the road end and trailhead (see the map for Hike 44).

Beginning at 1,800-feet elevation, the trail climbs gradually for 2 miles. The first mile follows a long-abandoned road to a trail junction. Staying right, you'll climb a few hundred feet, but then the trail levels out as it angles into the Milk Creek Valley and starts upstream alongside Milk Creek.

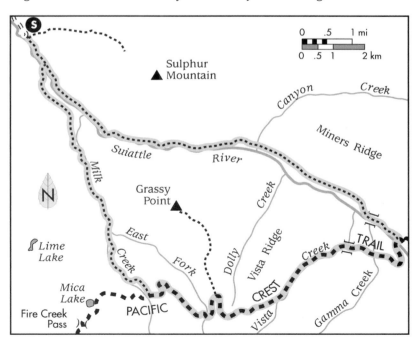

Vanilla leaf blooms along the Suiattle River Trail.

If you think the first 4 or 5 miles of trail are gentle—gaining just 1,000 feet—the next few start to wear you down. At 7.5 miles, you've finally gained 2,800 feet to reach the PCT. Turn north and you'll soon think the previous 7.5 miles was a cakewalk.

The first 4 miles of hiking on the PCT weave through dozens of tight switchbacks as the trail leads you up to a high, meadow-covered ridge with wonderful views of Fire Mountain, Kennedy Peak, and Glacier Peak. You've now topped out at 6,000 feet. A long traverse over the crest of Milk Ridge and around the meadows in the headwater basin of East Milk Creek brings you down to the camps scattered along Vista Ridge at 5,500 feet (about 14 miles from the trailhead).

The PCT crosses over Vista Ridge and descends sharply into the Vista Creek Valley. Here it starts to leave the meadows that it has followed since cresting the ridge above Milk Creek. But as you descend the last of the meadows, look north through the Vista Creek Valley to Miners Ridge and Plumbers Mountain far beyond.

The trail follows the creek north, dropping toward the upper Suiattle

River Valley. Campsites can be found at several locations along Vista Creek, with the best near the bridge at the end of the valley. After crossing Vista, the trail slants east for 2 miles and then joins the Suiattle River Trail near Gamma Creek (21 miles from the start of the loop).

In the next mile, the trail crosses the Suiattle River on a high, stable bridge, and then it heads downstream, staying close to the river's edge for the last 10 miles to the trailhead.

46 LYMAN LAKE BASECAMP

Distance: 20 miles to Lyman Lake	
Hiking time: 2 to 4 days (minimum)	
High point: 6,000 feet	
Elevation gain: 2,700 feet	
Season: Mid-July through September	
Map: Green Trails Holden, No 113	
Land manager: Chelan Ranger District	

Lyman Lake, situated in a deep cirque on the eastern side of the Glacier Peak Wilderness Area, is the perfect location in which to establish a comfortable basecamp while exploring the beauty of the PCT. The lake is a broad, deep body of water, with a sizable population of pan-sized trout. Excellent campsites ring the lake, with views of the surrounding peaks, including Chiwawa Mountain—home to the Lyman Glacier which feeds the lake—and Bonzana Peak across the valley.

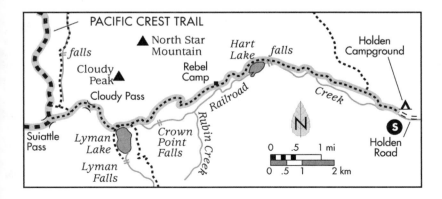

From the lake, a short jog up the trail gets you to the PCT, with explorations north and south just waiting to be enjoyed.

To get there, from Chelan take the *Lady of the Lake* ferryboat up Lake Chelan to Lucerne and then catch the shuttle bus to the community of Holden. Hike or hitchhike 1 mile up the Holden Road to Holden Campground and the official trailhead.

From the campground, the trail follows Railroad Creek upstream to Hart Lake. Just under a mile up the trail, a side trail leads north to Holden Lake. Stay to the left at the junction and continue along Railroad Creek as it meanders through the broad valley. Hart Lake, passed at about 3.5 miles, and Rebel Camp at 4.5 miles, both offer good campsites for those who get a late start up the valley. Make sure you use the provided bear cables to hang your food items.

At Hart Lake, the trail—still hugging the river—takes a sharp turn to the west. In 1 mile, just past Rebel Camp, veer uphill away from the river. The trail switchbacks up the steep slope to the 5,500-foot level before making a long traverse to Lyman Lake, elevation 5,696 feet.

There are fine camps along the lake's outlet stream. Even more campsites—less crowded—are near the head of the lake. A .75-mile trail climbs along the west side of the lake to Lyman Falls above the inlet to the lake.

Hikers taking a sun break on a ridge above Lyman Lake

After setting up camp, start your explorations. You might want to start by climbing the long, sloping meadows that lead to Spider Gap, up near Lyman Glacier to the south. These wildflower meadows extend from the lake all the way up to the 7,100-foot gap at the base of Spider Glacier. But this isn't the PCT. To explore the PCT, from the outlet stream rejoin the Lyman Lake Trail and turn left (west), hiking 1.5 miles through Cloudy Pass (6,400 feet) to a junction with the PCT at Suiattle Pass, elevation 5,983 feet.

Turning south on the PCT, descend through glorious meadows on the flank of Plummer Mountain, to a crossing of Miners Creek in 3 miles from the pass. From there, the PCT climbs to the crest of Middle Ridge in another 2 miles. Or, you can branch off the PCT onto Trail No. 789 just .5 mile south of Miners Creek and climb 2 miles to the alpine meadows on upper Middle Ridge and explore the lower slopes of Fortress Mountain.

Other options include heading north on the PCT from Suiattle Pass and following the meadows around the east flank of Sitting Bull Mountain—a 7,759-foot tower of rock above Agnes Creek. The PCT hugs the 5,500-foot level for nearly 5 miles north of the pass, offering a wonderful chance to explore the alpine meadows and marvelous views of this remote section of the Glacier Peak Wilderness Area. There are countless opportunities to explore off-trail in this area.

Return the way you came.

47 AGNES CREEK GORGE AND WEST FORK MEADOWS

Distance: Up to 15 miles round trip

Hiking time: 7 hours

High point: 2,300 feet

Elevation gain: 600 feet

Season: Mid-July through September

Map: Green Trails McGregor, No. 81

Land manager: Chelan Ranger District

The tiny community of Stehekin is nestled in a remote corner of the Cascades, sitting between the Glacier Peak Wilderness Area, the North Cascades National Park, and just within the Lake Chelan National Recreation Area. The only access to the community is via a long boat ride up Lake Chelan.

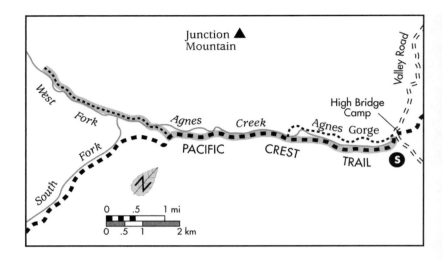

As remote as Stehekin is, this trail is even more remote, despite its short length. The trail explores a deep river canyon and miles of eons-old forest that tower overhead. Massive Douglas firs, ponderosa pines, cedars, and spruces fill the valley of Agnes Creek, and this trail weaves a gentle path through those forests, along the edge of the deep, thundering river gorge.

To get there, from Chelan take the *Lady of the Lake* ferryboat up Lake Chelan to Stehekin and ride the community shuttle bus up the Stehekin River Valley to the High Bridge Camp.

The PCT descends south from High Bridge Camp parallel to Agnes Creek. The creek, flowing north, has carved a deep, narrow cut into the volcanic rock of the valley. This gorge lies just west of the PCT, and you can frequently look into the churning chasm. When it's not in sight, the sound of the frothy waters thundering between the high walls fills the cathedral-like forest.

For 2.5 miles, the PCT parallels Agnes Gorge, slicing south through one of the most pristine and unique ancient forests left in the Pacific Northwest. Cedars 10 to 15 feet in diameter reside close by orange-trunked ponderosa pines and gnarly-barked Douglas firs standing 250 feet tall. The gorge is a thing of beauty, but the living forest transcends a concept as simple as physical beauty. The forest is a grand, ancient entity deserving, if not demanding, our respect and admiration. That these trees have stood in this valley even as the nearby gorge was being cut into solid rock is a testament to the enduring power of the natural world.

As the PCT continues south, the intensity of the gorge fades and soon the trail is paralleling a pretty wilderness stream and not a deep, rock-cutting torrent. But even in this milder form, the river is a thing of beauty, made even more beautiful a few miles up the trail as the old-growth forests begin to open onto sprawling forest glades and riverside meadows.

At the 5.5-mile mark, a side trail cuts west, crossing the creek. Head up this path and enter a broad valley whose floor is covered with acres of wildflowers on either side of the small stream—the West Fork Agnes Creek.

The towering forest of Agnes Grove

Explore at your leisure as the trail pushes 3 miles up the West Fork before returning to the main PCT and heading back northeast to High Bridge Camp.

48 STILETTO PEAK VIEW LOOP

Distance: 12 miles round trip	
Hiking time: 8 hours	
High point: 6,100 feet	
Elevation gain: 2,200 feet	
Season: Mid-July through September	
Maps: Green Trails Washington Pass, No. 50, and Stehekin, No. 82	
Land manager: Chelan Ranger District	

Feel free to customize your outing along this route. If you prefer to keep it easy and light, skip the climb to Stiletto Peak and instead simply enjoy the scenic, easy loop around the pretty Bridge Creek Valley. You'll find open, ancient forests with massive Douglas firs towering overhead and fruit-rich huckleberry bushes scattered between the trees.

To get there, drive the North Cascades Highway (SR 20) 1.5 miles east of Rainy Pass and park at the Bridge Creek Trailhead.

The small trail leads south and intercepts the PCT in just a few hundred yards. Turn left on the PCT and follow the wide valley of Bridge Creek. Looking up through the trees, try to spot Frisco Mountain to the west and, directly behind you, enjoy good views of Whistler Mountain. (Take just a few peeks back as you head out, knowing you'll be able to enjoy the view more fully on the return.)

About 1 mile south, the trail forks. Stay right on the PCT and cross the tumbling waters of Bridge Creek on, appropriately enough, a well-made bridge. For the next 3 miles, you'll follow the creek south and west as it contours around the base of Frisco Mountain. The trail stays in the trees but frequently comes within sight and sound of the creek.

Four miles from the trailhead, you'll find another junction at Fireweed Camps. This is a fine place to camp, and the short, easy hike to this camp makes it a good choice for a backpacking trip with youngsters.

At the junction, leave the PCT by turning left onto the McAlester Creek Trail. You'll pass three or four more camps in the next .5 mile

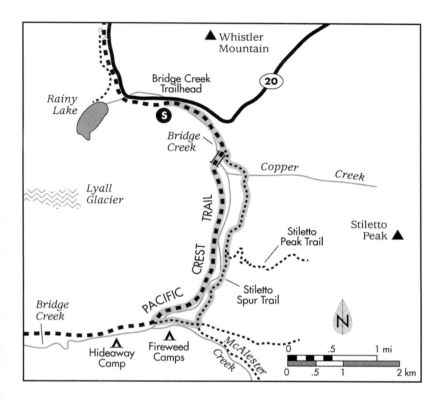

before hitting another trail fork. Go left again, this time on the Stiletto Spur Trail, and start back north along the Bridge Creek Valley, this time on the east side of the creek. After 1 mile of forest hiking, it will be time to make a decision. Stroll on back to the trailhead in the cool, refreshing forest, or trudge up a steep, 3-mile trail for unbelievable views of the North Cascade Peaks from a vast meadow on the flank of one of the mighty mountains.

The Stiletto Peak Trail cuts east from the main trail, climbing 2,100 feet in 3 miles of nonstop switchbacks. The trail leaves the forest and enters a broad sweep of meadows as it nears the upper end of the path, and finally the meadows give way to fields of rock as the trail ends directly below the 7,660-foot Stiletto Peak. Looking out from the mountain, enjoy views of Frisco, Hock, Whistler, and Twisp Mountains, among a score of other unnamed peaks. When you've had your fill and used up the last of your film, descend the Stiletto Peak Trail back to Bridge

Creek and turn right (north) to return to the PCT junction 1 mile south of the Bridge Creek Trailhead.

Return the way you came.

Columbine growing near a stream alongside Fireweed Camp

49 STEVENS PASS TO RAINY PASS THRU HIKE

Distance: 117 miles one way

Hiking time: 9 to 11 days

High point: 6,050 feet

Elevation gain: 4,300 feet

Season: Mid-July through September

Maps: Green Trails Benchmark Mountain, No. 144; Glacier Peak, No. 112; Holden, No. 113; McGregor Mountain, No. 81; Stehekin, No. 82; and Washington Pass, No. 50

Land manager: Chelan Ranger District

This is the longest stretch of the PCT and, although you could break it up by hiking out at Stehekin, it's worth a week on the trail to enjoy this wild, remote region. By hiking the more than 100 miles—spending more than 10 days in the wilderness—you will get a bit of the feel of thru-hiking the entire PCT. The terrain also promotes that association with long-distance thru-hikers as this long section mimics the rolling action of the PCT along its entire course—climbing high onto rocky ridges, traversing the flanks of great mountains, and descending into deep river valleys. Weaving through two wilderness areas, a national recreation area, and a national park, this section of trail is remote and wild. Between Stevens and Rainy Passes, the PCT passes deep, glacier-fed lakes, crosses thousand-acre meadows, and enjoys views of the jagged peaks along the crest of the northern Cascades.

To get to the southern trailhead, from Skykomish drive east on US 2 to Stevens Pass. Continue to the east side of the pass and park in the large lot on the north side of the highway near an old, abandoned service station. The trailhead is found behind a large, blocky structure that serves as a power substation near the north edge of the parking lot. For the northern trailhead, drive the North Cascades Highway (SR 20) to Rainy Pass and park in the large trailhead parking lot at the pass.

From Stevens Pass, the trail climbs north into the Henry M. Jackson Wilderness Area, past Lake Valhalla and Lake Janus to the long, high ridge north of Grizzly Peak. The Pear Lake/Peach Lake Basin is reached after miles of high meadow tromping, and then it's on to Skykomish Peak and Dishpan Gap. The views just keep getting better as you hike north.

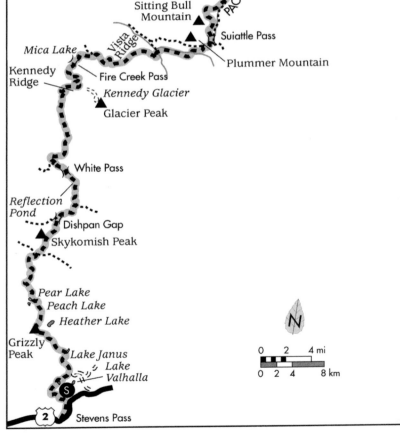

Rainy Pass Trailhead 20 S

Rainy Lake

Bridge Creek

Junction Mountain

High Bridge Camp

Creek

PACIFIC CREST TRAIL

Agnes

Sitting Bull Mountain

Suiattle Pass

Plummer Mountain

Mica Lake

Vista Ridge

Kennedy Ridge

Fire Creek Pass

Kennedy Glacier

Glacier Peak

White Pass

Reflection Pond

Dishpan Gap

Skykomish Peak

Pear Lake

Peach Lake

Heather Lake

Grizzly Peak

Lake Janus

Lake Valhalla

N

0   2   4 mi

0   2   4   8 km

S

2   Stevens Pass

Meadow along the PCT on the flank of Glacier Peak

Leaving Dishpan Gap, you'll find Glacier Peak looming ahead. You're soon within the Glacier Peak Wilderness Area and following a trail through the rocky alpine meadows along the west flank of the great volcano. Reflection Pond and White Pass are two highlights of the trail along the south side of the peak. Just after crossing White Pass, the PCT loops around White Pass, skirts Portal Peak, and climbs onto the rocky slopes of Glacier Peak proper. You'll hike next through a rocky cirque below White Chuck Glacier and through the flower-filled subalpine meadows of the Upper White Chuck River Valley.

A steep climb of Kennedy Ridge leads back to the meadows above timberline and for the next dozen miles, the trail stays in the high, alpine terrain. Fire Creek Pass, Mica Lake, East Fork Milk Creek, Vista Ridge, and meadows come and go as you stagger north in awe of the fabulous beauty all around the trail.

Once over Vista Ridge, the trail descends north away from Glacier Peak and enters the Suiattle River Valley and climbs to Suiattle Pass. A long descent down Agnes Creek leads to the High Bridge Camp, on the road above Stehekin about 97 miles north of Stevens Pass. This is your chance to bail off the trail, but with just 20 miles left to hike, it's worth it to continue on north.

From High Bridge—at 1,700 feet, the lowest point along this long stretch of the PCT—the trail follows Bridge Creek upstream nearly all the way to Rainy Pass, gaining more than 3,000 feet along the way. There are a host of excellent campsites established along the river. The last couple of miles of trail veer west away from Bridge Creek to ascend to Rainy Pass Trailhead.

50 CUTTHROAT PASS

Distance: 10 miles round trip

Hiking time: 6 hours

High point: 6,800 feet

Elevation gain: 2,000 feet

Season: Mid-July through September

Map: Green Trails Washington Pass, No. 50

Land manager: Methow Valley Ranger District

Dry, pine forests and larch-studded alpine meadows await you along the Porcupine Creek Valley. Hitting the trail in late summer, the meadows are

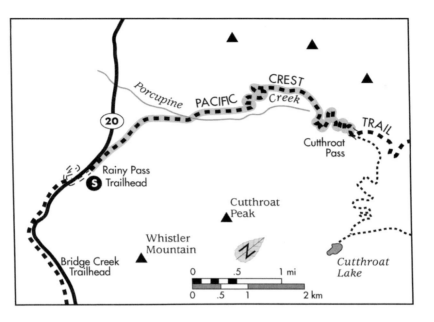

awash in color as the wildflowers rush to bloom in the couple of short months of summer that exist between the time when last year's snow all melted away and before new snow starts to fall. Hit the trail in early autumn—late September is the prime time—and you'll find the flower blooms long gone, but the plants' leaves will be brilliant orange and crimson and the thousands of larch trees will be deep gold.

To get there, drive the North Cascades Highway (SR 20) to Rainy Pass and park in the large trailhead parking lot at the pass.

Begin by finding the trailhead near the horse ramp at the west end of the parking lot. The trail curves west through a thin pine and fir forest, climbing gradually in the first mile as it rounds a ridge on the flank of Cutthroat Peak.

The forest begins to open as the trail climbs into the Porcupine Creek Basin and meadows start to show themselves, first on the slope opposite the trail, then around the trail itself. In 2 miles, the trail crosses the creek and climbs into the east-facing meadows on the slopes above the creek. This is where the views expand beyond the wonderful local scenery. Looking back to the southeast, you'll see the ragged, rocky top of 8,050-foot Cutthroat Peak. Larches and aspen give a golden hue to the slopes below the rocky summit from about mid-September to mid-October.

Within .5 mile of the creek crossing, the trail climbs a bit more steeply, swinging through a few long switchbacks to reach the 6,000-foot level. Now it's nothing but wildflower meadows and glorious views as you traverse the slope at this elevation for the next mile. But your eyes have been running up quite a bit of credit while feasting on the views during the long hike up the valley, and it's on the last mile to the pass that your legs and lungs pay off that debt.

View from the PCT near Rainy Pass

A long series of switchbacks ascends the final 800 feet up the headwall of the creek valley, finally cresting the ridge at 6,800 feet at the narrow saddle of Cutthroat Pass.

Now that your account is cleared, you are rewarded with a big bonus. Striking views abound as towering rock summits protrude into the sky in every direction you look. Pulling your eyes downward, the views are equally grand. Far below Cutthroat Pass, on the north slope of Cutthroat Mountain, is the blue gem of Cutthroat Lake. On all the slopes around you are vast meadows of wildflowers. Look closely and you might see deer, mountain goats, black bears, coyotes, marmots, pikas, golden eagles, red-tailed hawks, merlins, ospreys, or even peregrine falcons.

The PCT continues north toward Canada, but if you're a day hiker, turn around at the pass and enjoy the thrills of hiking down through those glorious meadows.

51 RAINY PASS TO HARTS PASS THRU HIKE

Distance: 31 miles one way

Hiking time: 3 days

High point: 6,900 feet

Elevation gain: 2,500 feet

Season: Mid-July through September

Maps: Green Trails Washington Pass, No. 50, and Mount Logan, No. 49

Land manager: Methow Valley Ranger District

Although much of the long PCT runs like a roller coaster up and down ridges, riding long ridge tops and descending into deep river valleys, this stretch is different. This leg of the PCT starts at one high pass, ends at another, and crosses five more passes in the 31 miles of its length. The trail hugs the ridges between each of those passes, never dropping into the valley bottoms. For 31 miles, the PCT lives up to its name in the truest sense—it straddles the crest of the Cascades, separating the wet, west-side forests of cedars and hemlocks from the dry, eastern forests of larch and pine.

To get to the southern trailhead, drive the North Cascades Highway

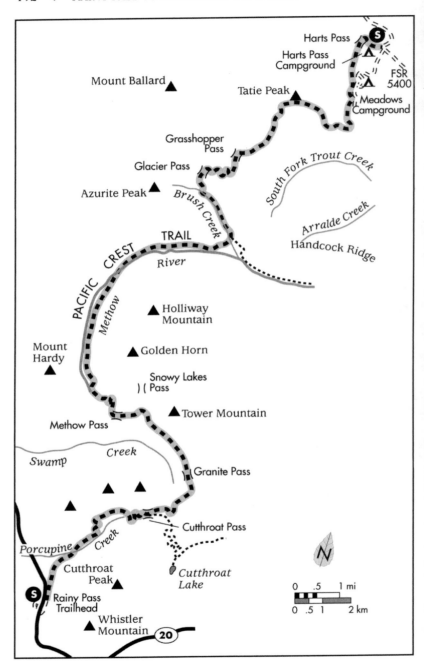

(SR 20) to Rainy Pass and park in the large trailhead parking lot at the pass. The northern trailhead is reached from Rainy Pass by continuing east on SR 20 to Mazama and turning left, crossing the river, and turning left again on Harts Pass Road (FSR 5400) at the Mazama Country Inn. Follow the road about 20 miles to its end at Harts Pass (elevation 6,200 feet).

Following the PCT north into the Porcupine Creek Basin, the trail soon leaves the forest behind and enters an enchanting world of alpine meadows dotted with larches and aspens, both of which turn a brilliant gold shortly after the first cold spell in early autumn. The PCT climbs Porcupine Valley to Cutthroat Pass and traverses north-

View down Methow River Valley from the PCT near Tatie Peak / Harts Pass

east around the rocky, steep slopes of an unnamed peak (7,552 feet) above Cutthroat Creek. About 7.5 miles from the trailhead, the PCT slants through its second mountain pass of this trip, Granite Pass at 6,200 feet.

On the south side of Granite Pass, the trail traverses above the dry-side forests of Cutthroat Valley, but just north of the pass, the trail hugs the headwall of Swamp Creek with its classic wet-side forests shrouded under a dark green canopy. Traversing the valley wall above the creek, you'll encounter the first good water and campsite 2 miles north of Granite Pass. One mile past that camp, the trail crosses its third pass.

Meadow-filled Methow Pass, at 6,600 feet, provides jaw-dropping views of Tower Mountain and the long line of rocky pinnacles on the ridge north of it, ending with Golden Horn (8,366 feet). Soak in the views, and then prepare for the one big descent along the route—a drop into the forested Methow Creek Valley. Fortunately, this is a high-country stream and the trail gets to just 4,400 feet before climbing the side valley cut by

Brush Creek to regain the Cascade Crest at Glacier Pass, about 21 miles north of Rainy Pass.

Glacier is a low pass, sitting at 5,500-feet elevation, and the PCT is a high-country trail, so from Granite Pass the trail turns vertical. A climb through 2 miles of switchbacks leads you back above treeline and into wildflower meadows at Grasshopper Pass, high above Trout Creek.

From Grasshopper (elevation 6,700 feet) the trail makes a long, northern traverse along the southern ridge of Tatie Peak before sweeping through the rocky cirque below the peak's summit and rambling gently north the last few miles through steep-sloping meadows to Harts Pass.

52 TATIE PEAK

Distance: 10 miles round trip	
Hiking time: 5 hours	
High point: 6,700 feet	
Elevation gain: 300 feet	
Season: Mid-July through September	
Map: Green Trails Washington Pass, No. 50	
Land manager: Methow Valley Ranger District	

This is a great day-hike for folks of all ages and abilities. You'll enjoy the marvelous high country of the North Cascades and the majesty of the PCT, but you won't have to struggle with a long climb to the ridge-top meadows. Why not? Because the trailhead is found at the end of the highest driveable road in the state. At 6,400-feet elevation, Harts Pass is the highest your car will ever get in Washington, and the trailhead is at the end of the road, at its highest point. But even if you had to climb a hundred switchbacks with a full backpack, this section of the PCT would be worth it. Starting in a straggling stand of larch and pine, the trail nestles among the wildflowers on a steep slope below a towering mountain peak. The views down the West Fork Methow River, and out over the North Cascade peaks, are unbeatable.

To get there, drive east on the North Cascades Highway (SR 20), east of Rainy Pass, to the small community of Mazama and turn left, cross the river, and turn left again on Harts Pass Road (FSR 5400) at the Mazama Country Inn. Follow the road about 20 miles to its end at Harts Pass

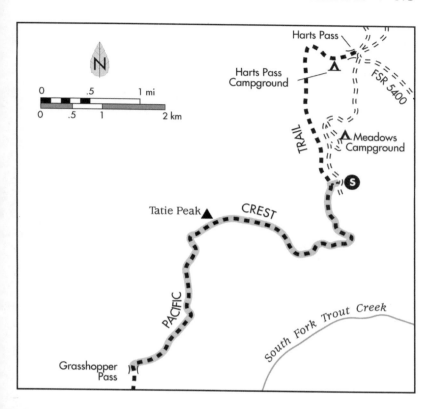

(elevation 6,200 feet). At the pass, stay left and drive south 1 mile past Meadows Campground to the southern end of the road.

Hike about 20 yards west through the trees and catch the PCT at the start of the meadows. Stay left and follow the trail south around the circular headwall of the North Fork Trout Creek Valley. The first mile of trail traverses this rocky wall, with spectacular views east into the valley. Below the trail, the wall slopes down through a talus field into a grove of golden larches. Above the trail, the north shoulder of Tatie Peak rises sharply to the west.

In about 1 mile, the trail swings around a sharp switchback through a shallow saddle and begins the long, easy traverse of the southern face of Tatie Peak. The terrain around the trail is now rockier with less vegetation, but the views are grander than those of the first mile. Looking over the South Fork Trout Creek Valley, you'll see the long side of Handcock

Ridge to the south and the hanging glaciers of Azurite Peak (7,957 feet) to the southwest. The trail crosses a steep slope near the 2-mile mark directly under the summit crown of Tatie Peak before tapering south into gentler slopes and greener meadows. Leaving the peak beyond, the trail continues south another 3 miles to Grasshopper Pass.

Here the meadows seem endless as they stretch out in all directions, but as pretty as the flower fields are, it's the panoramic vistas that make this pass special. To the west, Azurite Peak anchors the southern end of a long line of rocky pinnacles, with the northern end of the ridge held down by Mount Ballad (8,301 feet). The many unnamed peaks along the crest of Handcock Ridge lie to the south, and far beyond them are Golden Horn and Tower Mountain.

Explore the meadows around the pass, enjoy a picnic among the flowers, and then return to the trailhead the way you came, soaking in the views of Tatie Peak and the mountains to the north.

53 WINDY PASS

Distance:	7 miles round trip
Hiking time:	5 hours
High point:	6,900 feet
Elevation gain:	500 feet
Season:	Mid-July through September
Maps:	Green Trails Washington Pass, No. 50, and Pasayten Peak, No. 18
Land manager:	Methow Valley Ranger District

Enjoy some of the most scenic high country found along the 2,600-mile PCT without the trouble of having to climb a steep trail to see it. This section of the trail takes advantage of the high-elevation trailhead at Harts Pass and heads north through the endless fields of flowers in the alpine meadows of the North Cascades.

To get there, drive east on the North Cascades Highway (SR 20), east of Rainy Pass, to the small community of Mazama and turn left, cross the river, and turn left again on Harts Pass Road (FSR 5400) at the Mazama

The PCT along the flank of Tatie Peak

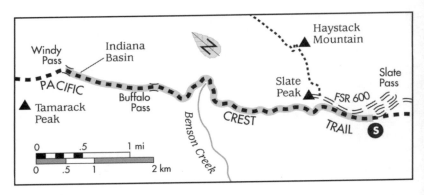

Country Inn. Follow the road about 20 miles to its end at Harts Pass (elevation 6,200 feet). Stay right when the road forks at the pass (the left fork leads into Harts Pass Campground) and drive up Slate Peak Road (FSR 600) 1.5 miles to the trailhead, found at the apex of the first switchback above Harts Pass. If you decide to take advantage of the Harts Pass Campground to spend a few nights in the high country, you can then skip the drive to the upper trailhead and catch the PCT as it crosses the road at Harts Pass. This adds 3 miles to the round-trip distance, but it's an easy, relatively flat 3 miles.

The PCT angles up through the meadows surrounding the trailhead for about .5 mile before leveling off for a rambling traverse around Slate Peak. As the trail heads north of Slate, it contours around the head of Benson Basin, which has apparently been ravaged by would-be miners. The grassy meadows are scarred with mounds of dirt and old roads. Moving north past the miners' mess at Benson Basin, the trail rounds a small, unnamed peak and then crosses Buffalo Pass. Pause here for views east of pristine, untrammeled meadows and, in all directions, majestic, snow-capped mountains. Tamarack Peak, to the west, is the most prominent, with its summit only a couple of miles away as the crow flies. Hiking north, Tamarack is now constantly in view, and when you reach Windy Pass, the peak seems close enough to touch—and it almost is. If you are an adventure-seeker, scramble through the meadows west of Windy Pass onto the slopes of Tamarack. If you are somewhat less adventurous, just sit at the pass and revel in the wonderful views. With Tamarack filling the horizon due west, cast your eyes out in any other direction to see more striking mountains. Jim Peak, Pasayten Peak, Wildcat Mountain, Haystack Mountain, and Azurite Peak are just a few of the craggy summits that litter the rugged North Cascades.

Stay and play in the meadows before retracing your steps to the trailhead.

A hiker on the PCT near Windy Pass buttons up as a storm sweeps into the North Cascades.

54 SEVEN-PASS LOOP

Distance: 27-mile loop	
Hiking time: 3 days	
High point: 6,800 feet	
Elevation gain: 2,000 feet	
Season: Mid-July through September	
Maps: Green Trails Washington Pass, No. 50, and Pasayten Peak, No. 18	
Land manager: Methow Valley Ranger District	

From Harts Pass, you'll cross Buffalo Pass, Windy Pass, Foggy Pass, Jim Pass, and Holman Pass as you head north, and on the return south you'll skirt Slate Pass before returning to Harts Pass. But even with so many passes to pass, the trail lacks a lot of strenuous up-and-down hiking. It helps that the trailhead is at Harts Pass, elevation 6,200 feet—you start high and stay up for the first half of the route. Following the PCT north to Holman Pass keeps you near the 6,000-foot level. Along the way, you'll cross rocky alpine meadows in the shadow of jagged granite spires. You'll hike under the boughs of old larch forests—venture up here in September to enjoy the awesome splendor of the larches as they don their golden mantles of autumn—and wander through broad fields of wildflowers.

To get there, drive east on the North Cascades Highway (SR 20), east of Rainy Pass, to the small community of Mazama and turn left, cross the river, and turn left again on Harts Pass Road (FSR 5400) at the Mazama Country Inn. Follow the road about 20 miles to its end at Harts Pass (elevation 6,200 feet). Park in the trailhead parking lot near the crest of the pass.

Heading north, the trail climbs modestly for the first 2 miles, ascending to the 6,800-foot level on Slate Peak before easing into a long traverse around the peak's flank. In another mile, cross the first of the six passes you'll hike over (the seventh being Harts Pass where you started the journey). Buffalo Pass is a low divide on the ridge separating Benson Creek Basin from the West Fork Pasayten River. Look west for some fine views into Allen Basin Park and down the Benson Creek Valley while you enjoy fabulous meadows in the pass itself.

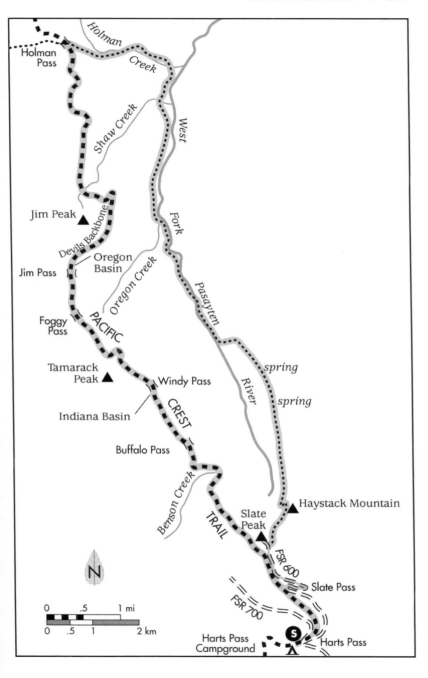

Holman Creek

Holman Pass

Shaw Creek

West

Jim Peak

Devils Backbone

Fork

Jim Pass

Oregon Basin

Oregon Creek

Pasayten

Foggy Pass

PACIFIC

Tamarack Peak

spring

River

Windy Pass

spring

Indiana Basin

CREST

Buffalo Pass

Benson Creek

Haystack Mountain

Slate Peak

TRAIL

N

FSR 600

0 .5 1 mi
0 .5 1 2 km

Slate Pass

FSR 700

Harts Pass Campground

Harts Pass

Although Buffalo is the first pass, you'll soon see that it isn't the best. The next pass to get past is Windy Pass on an east-reaching ridge of Tamarack Peak. Windy offers incredible views of the North Cascades' spires and peaks. The meadow-lined pass looks northeast to Gold Ridge and south to Haystack Mountain.

Rounding the eastern flank of Tamarack Peak, the PCT continues north on the ridge above the West Fork Pasayten River. As the trail approaches Jim Peak, it drops through the saddle of Foggy Pass and, 1 mile later, Jim Pass before cruising through deep green meadows in the Oregon Basin. Camps here are spectacular.

Now on the flank of Jim Peak, the PCT cuts east to avoid the jagged line of rock known as the Devils Backbone before slanting west once more around the north side of Jim. More campsites are found here as the trail crosses the headwaters of Shaw Creek near the 5,300-foot level.

A steep climb to the ridge top at 6,100 feet is followed by another descent through a long series of forested switchbacks to Holman Pass, 14 miles north of the trailhead at Harts Pass.

You'll leave the PCT at Holman Pass by turning right onto a side trail (No. 472A) and descending along Holman Creek to its junction with the West Fork Pasayten River. In 2 miles, turn right on the West Pasayten Trail (No. 472) and hike upstream, heading south, alongside the stream. The trail climbs past several excellent campsites located near the trout-filled river.

After you've traveled about 7 miles from Holman Pass, the trail crosses the river and begins a long climbing traverse of the east valley wall. The trees give way to meadows, and then the meadows give way to trees. You'll pass several good water sources and fine campsites along the hillside as you approach the 6,400-foot level of Haystack Mountain at the head of the West Pasayten Valley. Hugging the rocky slopes below the summit, the trail climbs around the west side of the peak and follows the ridge line south to Slate Peak just .5 mile south. You'll find an old dirt road leading to the fire lookout site at the top of Slate Peak. Follow this road about 1 mile down, going through Slate Pass, to a trailhead at a large left-hand switchback. Jump off the road onto this trail and drop a few yards west to the PCT. Turn south and hike the final 1.5 miles to the trailhead at Harts Pass.

Tumbling water near Holman Pass

55 HARTS PASS TO CANADA THRU HIKE

Distance: 39 miles one way

Hiking time: 3 to 4 days

High point: 7,126 feet

Elevation gain: 3,300 feet

Season: Mid-July through September

Maps: Green Trails Washington Pass, No. 50; Pasayten Peak, No. 18; and Jack Mountain, No. 17

Land manager: Methow Valley Ranger District

It's only 31 miles to the border, but if you don't mind making an illegal border crossing into Canada, it's far easier to descend the 8-mile trail into Manning Provincial Park than to turn around and return to Harts Pass. Of course, if you'd rather stick to U.S. soil, the trail back to Harts does cross some of the most rugged, untouched country in the lower 48 states, and even a return trip to see it again wouldn't be all that bad on the eyes (but might wear a little long on the legs).

To get to the southern trailhead, drive east on the North Cascades Highway (SR 20), east of Rainy Pass, to the small community of Mazama and turn left, cross the river, and turn left again on Harts Pass Road (FSR 5400) at the Mazama Country Inn. Follow the road about 20 miles to its end at Harts Pass (elevation 6,200 feet). Park in the trailhead parking lot near the crest of the pass. The northern terminus is in Manning Provincial Park, British Columbia. Drive north through one of the legitimate border crossing stations and head east on the Trans-Canada Highway, No. 3 to Manning Park. The trailhead is found just past the hotels clustered around Allison Pass in the park.

Heading north from Harts Pass, the PCT stays high atop the ridge separating the West Fork Pasayten River Valley on the east from the assorted creek basins on the west. In the first 14 miles, you'll cross five different mountain passes and enjoy views of dozens of towering mountains and countless acres of sprawling wildflower meadows.

Heading north from Holman Pass, the trail passes under a rocky cirque in the upper Goat Creek drainage. Take the name to heart and keep a watchful eye on the rocks of the rock wall to the west and farther north along Holman Peak, and you might see some of the snowy

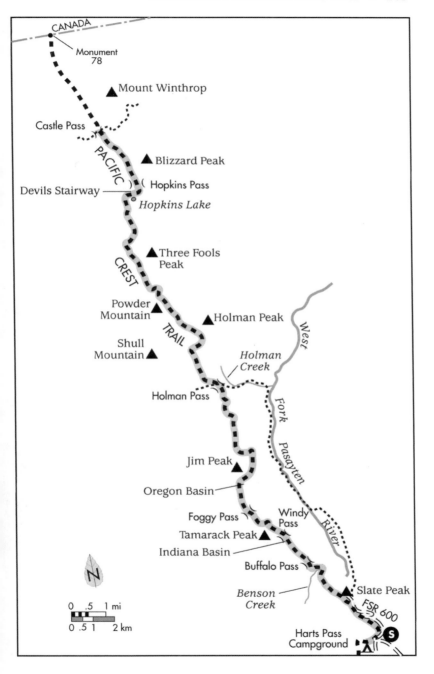

Golden larch in a valley near Windy–Holman Passes

white goats prancing across the sheer cliffs above the trail.

From the flank of Holman Peak, the PCT veers east along the ridge to Powder Mountain. From this point north, the trail stays in the high, rocky meadows of the alpine world. The spine of this ridge truly resembles a human spine with its protruding vertebrae. However, the ridge's protuberances aren't vertebrae but evenly spaced mountains. At the southern end is Holman Peak, then Shull Mountain, Powder Mountain, Three Fools Peak, Blizzard Peak, and Mount Winthrop, all in a row.

The trail passes some of the mountains on the east and some on the west, but it almost always stays above treeline. From Powder Mountain, the trail climbs over Woody Pass and descends past Three Fools Basin and its namesake peak to the excellent high-country campsites along Lakeview Ridge, just north of Three Fools Peak. The ridge is named for a handful of lakes seen dotting the east slope below the trail. Although the lakes themselves aren't accessible, usually some water can be found in small springs and snowmelt catch basins atop the ridge.

The trail crosses a small knob on the ridge at 7,100 feet—stop and slowly turn 360 degrees to absorb the awesome spectacle of being completely surrounded by wild alpine country—before you descend to the saddle above Hopkins Lake. From there, it's a grueling knee-pounding descent down the Devils Stairway to Hopkins Pass, at 6,100 feet.

The next 7 miles are all downhill, with views diminishing with every step. Dropping down the slope of Blizzard Peak, the trail hits Castle Pass 3 miles north of Hopkins, and then keeps dropping through forests to the 4,400-foot level in another 4 miles. At this point, you'll notice a long, straight band of greenery that breaks the seemingly continuous forests. In the middle of the band is a stone marker—Monument 78. This is the border between the United States and Canada—crews from both countries regularly clear the swath to ensure that the boundary line stays well delineated.

Although it's technically illegal to cross the border except at regulated border stations, it's highly unlikely that the Mounties will hunt you down, so continue north on the Castle Creek Trail to its end at Allison Pass.

APPENDIX A

LAND MANAGERS

Listed below are the addresses, phone numbers, and websites of the agencies that manage the Pacific Crest Trail. Contact the land managers before you head out for any trip to get the latest information on trail and weather conditions, and report any problems or hazards you encounter on the trails to those same land managers so they can get them fixed.

Okanogan National Forest
Forest Headquarters
1240 2nd Avenue South
Okanogan, WA 98840-9723
(509) 826-3275
www.fs.fed.us/r6/oka

Early Winters Visitor Information Center
North Cascades Highway 20
Mazama, WA 98833
(509) 996-2534 (summer only)

Methow Valley Ranger District, Twisp Office
P.O. Box 188
502 Glover Street
Twisp, WA 98856
(509) 997-2131

Mount Baker / Snoqualmie National Forest
Forest Headquarters
21905 64th Avenue West
Mountlake Terrace, WA 98043
(425) 775-9702
www.fs.fed.us/r6/mbs

View of Mount Adams from the north section of the Mount Adams Thru Hike, nearing Potato Hill

Darrington Ranger District
1405 Emmens Street
Darrington, WA 98241
(360) 436-1155

North Bend Ranger District
42404 Southeast North Bend Way
North Bend, WA 98045
(425) 888-1421

Skykomish Ranger District
74920 Northeast Stevens Pass Highway
Skykomish, WA 98288
(360) 677-2414

Verlot Public Service Center
33515 Mountain Loop Highway
Granite Falls, WA 98252
(360) 691-7791 (summer only)

White River Ranger District
857 Roosevelt Avenue East
Enumclaw, WA 98022
(360) 825-6585

Gifford Pinchot National Forest
Forest Headquarters
P.O. Box 8944
6926 East Fourth Plain Boulevard
Vancouver, WA 98661-7299
(360) 750-5000
www.fs.fed.us/gpnf

Mount Adams Ranger District
2455 Highway 141
Trout Lake, WA 98650-9724
(509) 395-3400

Cowlitz Valley Ranger District
Packwood Office
13068 U.S. Highway 12
Packwood, WA 98361-0559
(360) 494-0600

Wind River Ranger District
MP 1.23 Hemlock Road
Carson, WA 98610-9725
(509) 427-3200

Wenatchee National Forest
Forest Headquarters
215 Melody Lane
Wenatchee, WA 98801-5933
(509) 662-4335

Chelan Ranger District
Route 2, Box 680
Chelan, WA 98816
(509) 682-2576

Cle Elum Ranger District
803 West 2nd Street
Cle Elum, WA 98922
(509) 674-4411

Lake Wenatchee Ranger District
22976 State Highway 207
Leavenworth, WA 98826
(509) 763-3103

Naches Ranger District
10061 U.S. Highway 12
Naches, WA 98937
(509) 653-2205

North Cascades National Park
Ross Lake National Recreation Area
Lake Chelan National Recreation Area
Park Headquarters
2105 Highway 20
Sedro Woolley, WA 98284
(360) 856-5700
Emergency: (360) 873-4655 or 873-4590
www.nps.gov/noca

Golden West Visitor Center
Stehekin, WA 98852
(360) 856-5703, extension 340

Lake Chelan National Recreation Area
P.O. Box 549
Chelan, WA 98816
(509) 682-2549
www.nps.gov/lach

ADDITIONAL INFORMATION RESOURCES

Washington Trails Association
1305 Fourth Avenue, Suite 512
Seattle, WA 98101-2401
(206) 625-1367
www.wta.org

The Mountaineers
300 Third Avenue West
Seattle, WA 98119
(206) 284-6310
www.mountaineers.org

Pacific Crest Trail Association
5325 Elkhorn Blvd. PMB 256
Sacramento, CA 95842
1-888-PCTRAIL (728-7245)
www.pcta.org

Outdoor Recreation Information Center
REI Building
222 Yale Avenue North
Seattle, WA 98174
(206) 470-4060

APPENDIX B

SPENDING A DAY AS A TRAIL VOLUNTEER

In the 1998 season, the Washington Trails Association (WTA) achieved a goal many in the organization thought was unreachable—coordination of more than 41,000 volunteer hours! One year later, that number was pushed to 45,000 hours. That number represents the total accumulated efforts of volunteers during 300 days of work, including 18 week-long work parties.

WTA volunteer crews will continue to put in such efforts. In the coming years, work parties will go out every week of the year, and in the peak summer months, parties will go out five days a week with as many as eight events scheduled for each weekend. Plenty of opportunities will be available for anyone and everyone who is willing to help out. No experience is necessary, just a desire to work with some great people, have some fun playing in the dirt, and contribute to a cause that benefits all of us.

WHAT YOU NEED

WTA provides volunteers with tools, hard hats, and plenty of work to do, but if you want to help out, you need to be prepared. This means being properly dressed. The right clothes are necessary for your safety, and WTA emphasizes safety. When you arrive for a work party, please be wearing the following work clothes:

- A sturdy pair of boots. Standard hiking boots are fine, but tennis shoes are not.
- A pair of long pants (no shorts).
- A long-sleeved shirt (required).
- Work gloves.

WTA follows U.S. Forest Service standards for safety and work procedures, and therefore WTA cannot allow you to work if you are not properly dressed. Please also bring along a lunch, water, and snacks, but don't be surprised if goodies are passed around throughout the day.

Lookout Tower at the summit of Red Mountain, at the southern end of the Indian Heaven Wilderness

PLEASE BE ON TIME

All WTA work parties start at 8:30 A.M., and it's crucial to be at the trailhead and ready to go by that time. The crew leader will start off with a tool and safety lecture and an explanation of what you will be doing on the trail that day. Everyone must be present for the safety lecture to be allowed to work that day. No matter how many times you've heard it, you must be present for the lecture every time in order to work. When you sign up, WTA will send you information with directions to the trailhead and an estimated travel time.

WORKING

Before hitting the trail, the crew leader will divide up the work party into groups of five or six people, each headed by an assistant crew leader. Assistant crew leaders are more experienced volunteers who will show you the tricks of trail maintenance. Many different tasks are available, and which of the tasks you do depends on your level of experience or energy. We need people to cut brush, saw limbs, retread trail, and build drainage structures. Don't worry if you haven't had any experience working on trails, we love introducing new people to the joys of trail maintenance.

RESTING AND RELAXING

It doesn't matter how hard you work, you're not going to get paid! The crew leaders don't want you to work too hard (and they don't want to work too hard themselves), so each workday features at least one midmorning break. Crews also regroup for a long lunch together. This is the best way to get to know the people you're working with. People usually slow down a little after lunch and take a break or two before heading back down the trail, but please remember that the best time to take a break is when you want to. Crews typically return to the trailhead by 3:30 P.M., where you'll find snacks and beverages awaiting you.

WTA'S WORK PARTY EXTRA TEN ESSENTIALS

1. Sturdy boots
2. Long pants
3. Long-sleeved shirt
4. Work gloves
5. Rain gear

6. A lunch and snacks
7. Plenty of water
8. A good eye toward safety for yourself and your co-workers
9. Either a positive attitude or a goofy sense of humor (we accept both)
10. Ear-plugs if you're on a work party with Greg "The Goofer" Ball (WTA's Director of Operations and Chief Crew Leader)

We hope to see you on one of our volunteer work parties soon!

To sign up, or for more information on the WTA, call (206) 625-1367, or visit the WTA website at *www.wta.org*. For information about trail projects on the PCT in Oregon or California, contact the Pacific Crest Trail Association at (916) 349-2109 or visit the organization's website at *www.pcta.org*.

—*Washington Trails Association*

INDEX

ABOUT THE AUTHOR

Dan A. Nelson is executive editor of *Signpost for Northwest Trails*, a monthly backcountry recreation magazine published by the Washington Trails Association (WTA). He authored *Snowshoe Routes: Washington* (The Mountaineers Books, 1998) and was the writer and editor for the WTA-authored *Accessible Trails in Washington's Backcountry: A Guide to 85 Outings* (The Mountaineers Books, 1995). Nelson is also co-author of *Pacific Northwest Hiking: The Complete Guide to 1,000 of the Best Hikes in Washington and Oregon*. He is an outdoor recreation feature writer and columnist for *The Seattle Times* Outdoors and Travel sections, as well as a frequent contributor to *BACKPACKER* magazine. An avid hiker, backpacker, skier and snowshoer, Nelson has explored and photographed wilderness areas throughout the West. He lives in Puyallup, Washington.

Photo by Donna Meshke

THE MOUNTAINEERS, founded in 1906, is a nonprofit outdoor activity and conservation club, whose mission is "to explore, study, preserve, and enjoy the natural beauty of the outdoors . . . . " Based in Seattle, Washington, the club is now the third-largest such organization in the United States, with 15,000 members and five branches throughout Washington State.

The Mountaineers sponsors both classes and year-round outdoor activities in the Pacific Northwest, which include hiking, mountain climbing, ski-touring, snowshoeing, bicycling, camping, kayaking and canoeing, nature study, sailing, and adventure travel. The club's conservation division supports environmental causes through educational activities, sponsoring legislation, and presenting informational programs. All club activities are led by skilled, experienced volunteers, who are dedicated to promoting safe and responsible enjoyment and preservation of the outdoors.

If you would like to participate in these organized outdoor activities or the club's programs, consider a membership in The Mountaineers. For information and an application, write or call The Mountaineers, Club Headquarters, 300 Third Avenue West, Seattle, Washington 98119; (206) 284-6310.

The Mountaineers Books, an active, nonprofit publishing program of the club, produces guidebooks, instructional texts, historical works, natural history guides, and works on environmental conservation. All books produced by The Mountaineers are aimed at fulfilling the club's mission.

Send or call for our catalog of more than 300 outdoor titles:

The Mountaineers Books
1001 SW Klickitat Way, Suite 201
Seattle, WA 98134
800-553-4453
mbooks@mountaineers.org
www.mountaineersbooks.org